The
CONNECTION
COLLECTION
Relationship Centered Training Articles

SUZANNE CLOTHIER

ELEMENTAL ANIMAL, INC.

St. Johnsville, New York

Suzanne Clothier/Elemental Animal, Inc.
PO Box 105
St. Johnsville, NY/13452
www.SuzanneClothier.com

Publisher's Note: Much of the material contained in this work first appeared in articles available at the author's website and/or in her seminar handouts.

Book Layout © 2014 BookDesignTemplates.com

The Connection Collection/Suzanne Clothier – 10 9 8 7 6 5 4 3
ISBN 978-0-9765489-6-6

Dedicated to the countless animals who work so hard
to help me understand a bit more every day

The fidelity of a dog is a precious gift demanding
no less binding moral responsibilities
than the friendship of a human being.
KONRAD LORENZ

CONTENTS

Foreword

Much of what is contained in this book has appeared in various forms on my website and in my seminar handouts. Enough kind people prevailed on me to put this collection together and went further to provide real assistance to make the idea become reality. I thank them for their encouragement.

For what it's worth, many of the articles are available for free, in somewhat different format. (See my website for more information.)

I've selected writings that help frame out the bones of my Relationship Centered Training™ (RCT) approach. As you'll see, RCT focuses first and foremost on the dog while keeping the relationship between dog and handler truly central in all ways possible. I've tried to provide chapters that give both practical information and food for thought.

RCT is a common sense approach, full of ideas you may already understand from your life experience with humans. I hear this a lot. "Well, that's so simple. I knew that! Why didn't I know that for me and my dog?" Sometimes, my job is just to remind people of what they already know—and hang out with dogs. It's a great job!

A few notes to the reader: Yes, I know that dogs come in both male and female varieties. Unless referring to a specific dog with a specific sex, I'll refer to dogs as *he*. I've already apologized to all the female animals I live with; they didn't seem to care.

Handler is my generic term for the person trying to help the dog, work with him, deal with him, live with him. And yes, I also know that, like dogs, handlers come in different sexes. I am one of the other kind, myself.

While I could explain a lot using terminology, and I recognize that terminology has its place in discussions among those interested in the arcane details of behavior, learning theory, and more, I have chosen not to use that language here. Instead, I hope to provide you with a thoughtful exploration using language and examples that are clear, simple, and readily understood. Simple never means simplistic, as the "simple" creatures around me remind me every day.

In this collection, I trust you'll find a few gems that will help you in your relationship with dogs and any other animals.

See the dog. Always…

Suzanne Clothier
Hawks Hunt Farm, St. Johnsville, NY
January, 2015

CHAPTER ONE

What Is RCT— Relationship Centered Training™?

Three Core Concepts and Nine Keys form the RCT framework

Relationship Centered Training (RCT) is not a system for training animals. It is a framework for a life shared with dogs and other animals. RCT places *the relationship* between human and dog at the center of all you do. All else—training methods, equipment, training gurus, hopes and dreams—are evaluated, and then accepted or rejected, based on their effect on the relationship between you and your dog.

Rather than focus on telling you that you must always use this method or that particular equipment, or that you should never do X, Y, or Z, RCT asks you: "What kind of relationship do you want with your dog?" This fundamental question has a profound effect on all you do.

For the thinking trainer, RCT has great appeal. Its framework provides a powerful way to effectively sort the bewildering range of information about training and behavior.

For example, trainer X says you must always use Equipment A. Yet, each time you approach your dog with this equipment, he avoids you, ducks his head. With the equipment on, he flattens his ears, drops his tail. He makes it as clear as he can that this does not work for him, no matter what your instructor says. "Pay no attention to that," says the instructor. "He'll get used to it."

Uncomfortable, you accept the advice, lacking any way to sort it as good or bad or helpful. You tell yourself that you don't understand dog training, that the instructor must know because she has many ribbons and attends many seminars, and that this must be part of how experts train their dogs.

With the RCT framework in your pocket, you can ask yourself if this kind of interaction between you and your dog is what you hope for, if your dog's body posture and emotional state are what you want. Chances are good that the answer would be: "I don't want that for me and my dog." RCT provides the awareness that helps you sort advice as suitable or not suitable for you and your dog.

For example, you could ask for different equipment that doesn't have the same effect on your dog. A good trainer knows many ways to achieve the same results and should be able to offer you alternative equipment or techniques. If you didn't get satisfactory answers, you could recognize that this instructor and that method were not a good fit for you and your dog.

RCT offers a way to intelligently think about the choices you make for yourself, your dog, and the relationship. Here is a brief look at the different elements involved in RCT so that you can identify your strengths and challenges.

While these are simple concepts, they are not simplistic. The joy and the journey lies in learning to live these concepts and applying them in every day life awareness and diligence is a day by day process, a journey to be lived.

The RCT framework is built on three Core Concepts and nine Keys:

- **Connection**
  - Heartfelt
  - Awareness
  - Respect

- **Communication**
  - Information
  - Feedback
  - Consequences

- **Commitment**
  - Attention
  - Responsibility
  - Trust

CONNECTION
Heartfelt

Key to RCT is the concept of a *heartfelt* connection. When a relationship is heartfelt, there is a connection not only mind-to-mind but also heart-to-heart. This is deeply emotional, and each in the relationship wants to be with the other. There is joy and love in the connection.

The heartfelt aspect of a relationship cannot be taught, though handlers can be helped to understand their dogs and their relationships in new ways. It can be upsetting to care about dogs but be angered, frustrated, annoyed, or even frightened by them. Sometimes, people are simply disappointed by a dog who doesn't live up to their expectations.

RCT shifts the focus to the relationship and helps uncover aspects that are imbalanced or underdeveloped. Bringing these aspects into balance, strengthening them, and helping to resolve conflict can create profound shifts in the dog-human relationship.

Awareness

Awareness means consciously including the other in all that you do. Wherever you go, whatever you're doing, your dog remains a part of your consideration. And your dog maintains an awareness of you as well. When awareness is present, each of you notices the body language and actions of the other, and responds appropriately. This awareness is maintained *despite distractions*.

When you're with a dog, have a "crush" on him. Maintain a heightened awareness of where he is and what he's doing. Be super sensitive to him, and attentive to any shifts in his mood or posture.

RCT also expects the dog to maintain awareness of his handler. This expectation aligns well with the dog's basic nature; he is a social creature, and awareness of the social group is part and parcel of a dog's mind.

Respect

Respect means having reverence and regard for the other's needs, abilities, limits, and perspective. This is more easily said than lived in a moment-to-moment way.

Understand that the dog's perspective can be quite different from your own. He thinks differently than you and sees the world through very different senses. What is important to you may not be important to the dog, and vice versa. Respecting the differences is key to a healthy relationship.

Respect is earned, not forced or assumed. Dogs are very specific in giving precisely the respect you have earned. And they adjust it up or down according to changes in *your* behavior. This is very much like the respect you earn (or lose) in your human-to-human relationships.

One way to earn a dog's respect is through an ongoing commitment to working with the dog using the **Puppy Politeness Poker**™ (PPP) approach. This means asking the dog to work with you for the real life rewards that matter to him. That might be meals, play, coming in or out of the house, being released from his crate, or anything else the dog finds valuable and needs you to get for him.

Respecting the dog means that you understand his limits and abilities. What the dog doesn't know, he cannot do, no matter how much he respects you. Too often, failures in training are assumed to be due to a dog's lack of respect. If he is afraid, confused, or unsure, respect for you will not help him solve the situation; he needs skills, safety, and understanding. Respect does not equal skill or understanding or agreement.

A lack of respect *can* be seen in this common situation: the dog *does* know what to do but outright refuses to do it. If this is so, and the dog is not afraid, confused, overwhelmed, hurting, or bored, you may need to look hard at the balance of respect in the relationship. His refusal is a telling commentary.

COMMUNICATION

RCT views life with dogs as an ongoing conversation. RCT is a two-way street, with information coming to you from the dog, and from you to the dog.

Sometimes, the conversation is casual; sometimes it is much more formal, such as when we are teaching the dog specific skills or asking him to behave in certain ways. But, at all times, it is an ongoing conversation with a friend.

Most importantly, this is a conversation that takes place any-time you are with the dog. Training occurs when you are with the dog, whether you are deliberately focusing on teaching the dog or not. The dog believes that what you say and do are what you in-tend to say and do. That's how he acts—always aligned with his intentions and feelings in the moment. To such an honest creature, it's not conceivable that you might say or do things without mean-ing them. This creates an obligation for us to be in control of ourselves, aware of our intentions, and clear in what our words and deeds convey to a dog.

Information

In every conversation, information is important. When working with a dog, we use deliberate signals to communicate. Useful in-formation is timely, meaningful, and clear. Your dog needs you to have (or develop) good timing and a thoughtful, deliberate use of your body language, facial expressions, and tone of voice.

Whether you are pleased or displeased with him, you need to be clear so the dog can understand you. Your message needs to be meaningful to the dog. You also need to learn what your dog finds useful or confusing, overwhelming, or just right. You might want to give your dog pats to reward him, but the dog may pull back. He's telling you that your way of communicating "Good dog!" is not one he enjoys. Instead, he might appreciate a treat or a gentle stroke along his neck or a toss of his ball.

The dog, of course, is always giving us signals, whether we understand them or not. Understanding your dog means that you learn to "read" dog so that his signals (body language, vocalizations, and expressions) are clearly understood by you.

Feedback

Information alone is not enough. In a healthy relationship, information leads to feedback—a loop where you respond to your dog, and your dog responds to you, and you respond to your dog responding to you, and your dog responds to you responding to him responding to you, and so on.

In a good feedback loop, each responds with clear and prompt responses, altering behavior according to what the other has to say, looking for responses, readjusting, etc.

In a bad feedback loop, things go off track in any number of ways. You might respond to your dog too late for the information to be meaningful to him. You might overreact or underreact, responding with too much or too little. You might misunderstand and respond in a way that makes no sense to the dog. When he responds, based on what he sees as your nonsensical response that you think made sense to him, his response makes no sense to you. Then, your confused response to his confused response goes even further astray till everyone is frustrated, and you wonder, "Who's on first base?"

At every step, the goal is staying connected, clearly communicating, and being in balance with each other. In a good feedback loop, you're constantly making small adjustments to keep the relationship harmonious and strong. This is just like the way you make small adjustments when driving to keep you on the road and moving at the right speed, in the right direction. The quicker you recognize the need for and then make the adjustment, the smoother the journey.

Consequences

Because we often need to ask the dog to behave in certain ways (whether for his own good or because we have specific goals), we need to always consider the consequences of our communications. Simply put, consequences can either encourage or discourage the dog, or be neutral and have no deliberate effect.

If we like what a dog has done, the consequences we provide can encourage him to do it again. Praise, food rewards, play—all help encourage the dog. RCT focuses on the frequent and generous use of encouraging consequences.

If we do not like what a dog has done, we can discourage that in a number of ways: by not offering praise or food rewards, withholding attention or play, or using stronger consequences. RCT focuses on using discouraging consequences rarely and with great care.

Doing nothing leaves it up to the dog to decide whether he will or will not repeat a behavior. If he finds it enjoyable or necessary, he will probably do it again. By necessary, I mean that the dog may not enjoy behavior X but the situation forces that behavior, such as growling in response to being threatened by a person.

RCT emphasizes strongly encouraging the dog and using discouragement sparingly.

Whatever the consequence, it needs to be appropriate and fair for the situation. Consequences also need to be effective. Timeliness, clarity, and meaningfulness count.

This is not a one-way street. Dogs also provide us with consequences, as they are also interested in encouraging our behavior or discouraging our actions. Look for the ways your dog is encouraging or discouraging *you*.

Step into the dog's world. Use the "magic microphone" to interview the dog and get his perspective on the situation. It may be helpful to have a friend play your role while you play your dog's role. Try to "be the dog" in any given situation and guess at how it may be affecting him.

If you adjust your behavior according to what you imagine the dog is thinking and feeling, the dog will let you know if you're right or not. The "right" interpretation and solution will result in an improvement in the dog's response.

COMMITMENT

Healthy relationships require ongoing commitment. This is why we say that RCT is a way of life for living with dogs.

Attention

Consider this: How much connection and attention do you want and need from your dog? How much attention can you offer him? You cannot put the dog on hold, give scattered attention, or accept disconnection, and then, at certain times, decide you want complete connection and the utmost attention.

Connection must be practiced continually. Your commitment to being attentive and connected will help define how successful the relationship is for you and your dog.

Commitment means that you and your dog remain open to information, whenever it comes, in almost any circumstance (emergencies are exceptions). Both you and the dog remain receptive to each other's actions and directions, and are able to split your attention.

Just as a wise parent is committed to helping children learn to be polite in all situations, you need to be committed to helping your dogs learn how to maintain a high quality connection.

Responsibility

Keeping in mind that dogs are social animals, RCT asks that both human and dog take responsibility for their share in the relationship. I refer to this as *social responsibility*.

Just as we expect other people and children to learn and remember what polite behavior means, we can teach dogs to be responsible for their own behavior. This means actively participating without reminders. Many times, handlers take full responsibility for a dog's behavior, never asking him to be responsible. Other dogs, however, do expect the dog to be socially responsible. He's capable of it, and this can be taught.

Trust

Trust means having confidence in the other's ability and willingness to react appropriately, regardless of what's going on around them. Of course, we cannot trust anyone who has not yet learned what appropriate responses are. So, we have an obligation to help dogs understand what is right and what is wrong.

Trust also means that we are unafraid of the other and the other's intentions even when we (or they) are feeling confused or fearful, pressured, or distracted. For handlers, healthy relationships include trusting that the dog is trying to do his best.

In any given situation, the dog's behavior tells you what his best guess is as to how to handle the situation. If he had a better way to do things, he probably would. He is trying to keep good things happening and trying to keep bad things to a minimum, or, if he can, make them stop or go away. He wants to have fun, and he wants to avoid conflict. Just like you.

If you don't like his best guess, it's up to you to find a way to help him find another response. It's not about being dominant or submissive or pack order. It's about what the dog knows or doesn't know.

If you hear yourself saying, "But he knows better!" then consider this: if that *is* true, why would he not do it? He has a reason for refusing to cooperate. Trust that.

The trainer's job *always* is to figure out how to make it possible for the dog to cooperate. While a dog might be willing to cooperate, he can only be successful if he has the necessary skills. This seems like common sense, yet, many times, handlers forget to ask the simple question: "What skills does the dog need so he can succeed?"

If the dog is lacking the skills he needs, step one is training. Teach him what he needs to know. You cannot expect a dog to sit and stay while you open the front door if he doesn't know how to sit and stay. Identify the specific skills the dog needs in any given situation, and be sure you've actually taught him those skills.

If the dog has the necessary skills but is unable to put them to good use, some changes are needed. What might help the dog be successful in cooperating with you? Some options are lowering the expectation, decreasing the intensity of the situation, strengthening the skill itself through more practice, or improving the skill—or all of the above.

Other Considerations

Learning a new approach and techniques can be confusing and even scary at times. You may feel "stuck" not wanting to use the old ways but still not sure how to effectively use new techniques. Do your best, muddle through. Every day, and with every dog, it gets easier and easier. Some helpful hints:

- Love and kindness are wonderful, but they are not training.
- Understand training principles and theory. This helps you figure out why things go right or wrong, and why.
- Practice the technical training skills, such as handling, use of equipment, timing, and delivery of rewards. These skills are your communication skills.
- Balance is important. Avoid drowning in technical know-how and forgetting the heart and soul of relationship.
- Growing as a trainer requires forgiveness for yourself and your dog. Relationships include mistakes; learn from them.
- Don't be afraid to fail; know what you were trying for and how to analyze how/where/why it went wrong.

CHAPTER TWO

How Much Does Your Dog's Cooperation Weigh?

Physical struggles aren't the point in Relationship Centered Training

A few years ago, I began to realize that clients were constantly telling me how much their dogs weighed, but only the clients who were having trouble with their dogs. Those who had other concerns (such as canine athlete evaluations, jumping problems, specific training issues, and fine tuning performance) rarely if ever told me how much their dogs weighed. After thinking this over for a while, I was ready for the next client who told me how much her dog weighed—in this case, 75 pounds. I asked if she were married, which she was, and then asked, "How much does your husband weigh?" There was a long pause and then a rather icy reply, "That's none of your business."

I reassured her that I didn't actually care how much he weighed, that I was just curious if he weighed more than she did. She allowed that, yes, he did outweigh her. Then, I asked if she had any neighbors, which she did, and again asked how much they weighed. In the deep silence (annoyed silence, to be sure), I asked if she worked for others. If so, how much did they weigh? And the dry cleaner or mechanic she used—did they weigh more than she did? What about her friends?

Now she was just about sputtering in bewildered indignation, and no doubt wondering why she'd thought a phone consultation with me was a good idea, when I let her off the hook. "Do you stop to think about how much other human beings weigh when you try to work with them in any way?"

After a moment's thought, she responded that, of course, she didn't need to think about how much other people weighed when she wanted or needed their cooperation. She assumed that if she was reasonable and clear, they would be cooperative to the best of their ability. Unless we are in a physical confrontation with someone, our interactions with other humans are mostly about the communication/conversation we have with them, which does not usually include physical force.

I then asked if she had ever had moments when she had no awareness at all of how much her dog weighed. Had she experienced any moments of wonderful lightness when the dog's eyes were bright and he was attentive and working with her freely, happily, and not because she was hauling him around or holding him back?

With a smile in her voice, she said she *did* have those moments and loved them best of all. And that's what made it so frustrating to be dragged around by this dog, or hanging on to him for dear life at other times. I pointed out that any time she became aware of her dog's strength and weight, it was a clear signal that the connection was broken. In those moments, no training was going on. She was simply physically restraining him.

When the connection is clear and strong, there is no sensation of physically fighting or restraining the dog. Regardless of any being's size, *cooperation weighs nothing.*

Anytime you are aware how strong another being is and realize how much they weigh, it's probably because they are working *against* you and not *with* you. Some exceptions are: deliberately asking the dog to pull, as in tracking; doing protection work; playing tug games; when the dog climbs, sits, or lies on top of you; or having to restrain the dog for a veterinary procedure. Anytime you think, "Heavens, this dog is so strong!" it's probably time to back up and find a way to reconnect.

My goal as an instructor is to develop the connection so that the lead/collar simply becomes a safety device. I see the leash as a backup net for any mistakes that may be made, especially in places where there's no room for a mistake to be made safely. A leash can also be a way to deliver *soft* signals of guidance. And, of course, a leash may be compliance with local leash laws.

Training is not about the equipment. Good training is about the connection, the relationship, the cooperation.

The dog's willing cooperation weighs nothing. It is in those moments of connection that we find the "unbearable lightness of being"—then it becomes a dance of two minds and two hearts, and not a physical contest.

CHAPTER THREE

The Language of the Body

Recognizing messages in the dog's body language

This chapter is meant to give the reader some specifics of canine body language. It is not an exhaustive catalog of the astonishing range of expressions that dogs are capable of, and no handy-dandy illustrations or photos accompany the text. It is a brief guide to understanding which aspects of the dog's body language may be involved at different times, and what to look for.

The wide range of behaviors displayed by dogs are communications from the dog to us. Recognizing and respecting these communications is the foundation of a strong relationship with our dogs, but often, even the most loving handler can be confused, upset, or even threatened by the messages a dog sends.

If you are able to recognize early signs of a dog feeling uneasy or pressured in some way, you can avoid pushing the dog into feeling the need for dramatic or more dangerous aggressive behavior. Dogs do not snap, snarl, growl, or bite without reason, and those reasons can range from feeling afraid to being confidently challenging. Dogs also have good reasons why they shut down, withdraw, and become avoidant or resistant. No one who cares about a dog would want to deliberately push him into feeling unsure, unsafe, or afraid.

Body language is how an animal's internal state is expressed externally. Unlike your fellow humans, your dog can be trusted to tell you the truth about what he's feeling at any given moment. Like your fellow humans, your dog can be conflicted—and show it in his body language.

At the heart of all body language are fluctuations in arousal. Arousal can be good—happiness, joy, laughter, play. Or it can be unpleasant—anxiety, fear, panic. Body language reveals whether the dog is going up the spectrum towards activation or down the arousal spectrum to inhibition.

One side effect of increasing arousal, whether inhibition or activation, is the loss of fine motor control. This means that the dog's movements will lose smoothness, become jerky or abrupt, more rapid, or less coordinated. This can result in dogs taking treats or toys with a hard mouth; fine motor control is necessary for good bite inhibition.

Both activation and inhibition will have specific effects on the dog's body language, and these are detailed in the following sections.

Overall Geometry

While details matter a great deal, there are big overall messages that a dog can communicate with the geometry of his body posture—basic shapes to help us know about the dog's overall state of mind.

When a dog is relaxed, his body roughly forms a rectangle. The head and tail are held near or a bit above the level of the back. The tail may hang straight down, held in a relaxed position. If wagging, it will be soft wags that are neither quick nor hard. The stance the dog takes is also telling. The relaxed dog stands with the legs "one at each corner," very much like a table. It's safe to say that a dog who is in mental/emotional balance will reflect it in his physical balance, unless an injury or physical limitation prevents that normal stance.

When a dog becomes excited, his body begins to expand upwards. His head and tail begin to rise, with the tail now held at the level of the back or higher as his excitement grows. He literally looks taller, "up on his toes," and in fact he is standing taller due to an increase in muscle tension that extends right down to his toes. As the excitement increases, he may also begin to lean forward. The rectangle of the relaxed dog now becomes pulled forwards into a parallelogram.

When a dog becomes worried, fearful, unsure, or apologetic, his body compresses. His head and tail are held lower. The tail may be tucked and begin to wag in short quick wags, particularly if he is anxious. As the fear increases, the tail is tucked tighter and tighter to the body. The dog looks smaller than usual, and in fact he is, due to increased flexion in his joints as he compresses the overall posture.

As anxiety, fear or lack of confidence increases, the compression becomes more pronounced. He begins to leans backwards, away from whatever is concerning him. The balanced rectangle of the relaxed dog now becomes pulled backwards and down.

Speed and Quality of Movements

A relaxed, interested dog has smooth, easy movements of his eyes, head, ears, body, and tail. Take time to study your dog's face when he is calm. Notice how many small gestures there are even when he is relaxed, and pay particular attention to the quality and speed of those movements. Even if moving at speed, the quality of movement remains well coordinated and smooth in a confident, relaxed dog.

The inhibited dog is feeling worried, afraid, irritated or pressured. Along with the compression in his overall body language, he will also show slower movements in his body, eyes, head, and tail. Though he is feeling intense emotions, the effect of his arousal inhibits him. When the stress becomes overwhelming for him, he may stop moving altogether and freeze. Avoid pressuring the dog through verbal encouragement, repeated signals, or trying to interest the dog in food or toy rewards.

An activated dog who is irritated or aggressive may also show you slower movements in his body, eyes, head, and tail. But, with this dog, the slower movements are not due to inhibition but to increasing tension throughout his body as his irritation or anger increases. Along with the stillness comes warning signs: hard unblinking eyes, breath held, and stiffness throughout the body. A dog in this state is highly aroused and not afraid. Do not push this dog further or try to "win" in that situation. Quietly walk away from the situation.

When intensely activated or inhibited, the level of arousal will affect more than just body language; the dog may have trouble thinking clearly, making good decisions, or remembering rules. You may need to help him return to a more appropriate state of arousal by asking him to stand quietly near you until his movements are smooth and slow. As his arousal decreases, he will choose to sit and then lie down on his own. These volitional postural shifts are important clues to his arousal level.

If the dog is afraid or worried, removing him from that situation may be appropriate and allow his arousal to subside in the absence of triggering stimuli.

Curves

Curves are helpful clues to a dog's state of mind. Think about the last time you were greeted by a happy, friendly puppy. What you probably saw was a wriggling, curved body tumbling right towards you. These curves are deliberate gestures that, when combined with movement, indicate, "I am friendly!"

Puppies especially tend to use curves to indicate their friendliness, particularly as they are excited and making a direct approach. Without the curves, a rapid direct approach is quite rude and possibly threatening. With the curves, the message is mitigated to something along the lines of "I mean no harm, just excited!"

Sometimes the curves are seen in the whole body, but they may also be shown in smaller gestures, such as a curve through the head and neck, or a moderate curve in the ribcage. A true play bow contains many curves. When the dog is feeling playful or attracted to another dog or person, the curves tend to be towards that person or dog. When you become aware of curves, you'll begin to see them in many ways, big and small.

Curves *without* movement often indicate that the dog is feeling concerned, unsure, or afraid. For example, the dog who sees something scary or new, like the tough neighborhood cat staring him down. Typically, the dog will freeze, his body curving away from the scary kitty. When the dog feels worried or afraid about something, the curves in his body will tend to be held away from, not towards, the source of concern.

Straight Lines

Straight lines send a different message than curves do and can indicate a more serious state of mind. Straight lines can simply reflect confidence or, when combined with other details, part of a "keep your distance" threat.

A dog who is standing quietly with his body in a straight line oriented to you is feeling confident, unworried, unpressured. If you see that the dog is soft-eyed with his tail held low or near back height, with the tail wagging in big sweeps, then he is confident and friendly. Goofy dogs or adolescents might show the same overall picture but have a lot more wiggle and a bit less control of their posture.

Straight lines and direct orientation with no movement are a warning from the dog that you should keep your distance. Be particularly concerned if the tail is held high and moving only a little (if at all), and the dog is standing very straight and still. This is a serious warning from a confident dog. Do not approach a dog showing that behavior.

If you encounter a dog with this body language, give him a wide berth, or better still, quietly back away and leave the area.

Shifts in breathing

Shifts in the dog's arousal will be reflected in shifts in breathing such as:

- Regularity—a relaxed dog has an even rhythm to his breaths. As arousal increases, the rhythm can become irregular, even ragged.
- Depth—a relaxed dog takes full deep breaths at regular intervals. A worried dog can take shallow breaths, breathe at irregular intervals, or even hold his breath.
- Panting—a relaxed dog pants only to thermoregulate. Due to increasing arousal, a stressed dog is often panting long before any unstressed dogs in the same environment.

- Interruptions—a relaxed dog might interrupt his breathing briefly in order to listen to a sound or focus on something that has caught his eye. An irritated or aggressive dog might interrupt his breathing in order to close his jaw and offer a warning of stillness, however brief. Growls also interrupt breathing and, of course, may occur with an inhibited or activated dog.

Breathing may be monitored in a number of ways. Visual observation is easy and safe. Watch the dog's rib cage or flank area—a relaxed dog is visibly breathing with deep even breaths.

You may also be able to hear the changes in breathing, such as alterations in the rhythm, held breaths, panting, or quick shallow breathing. With a safe, non-aggressive dog, practice listening to breathing by closing your eyes and having someone else show the dog a cookie or a toy or something he finds very interesting. Without your helper telling you, can you detect when the dog's breathing tells you about the change in his arousal and attention?

If you are handling a dog, you may be too close to easily see changes, but you will be able to feel changes through your hands. The soft part of the flank along with the rib cage offers the best places for monitoring breathing changes. Obviously, handling a

potentially aggressive dog should be done with great care, but monitoring breathing while handling will help keep you safe while avoiding pushing the dog too far.

Changes in shape and expression of eyes

The facial muscles around the eyes, nose, lips, and muzzle all contain powerful connections to your dog's emotional centers in the brain. Changes in these areas are among the earliest signs that a dog's state of mind is changing.

Dogs are incredibly expressive in their eyes. The shape and expression of the eye can change considerably depending on the dog's state of mind.

The relaxed dog has a soft look and shape to his eye, with all the muscles around the eye also showing relaxation. The eyebrow is not prominent.

On the fearful/anxious end of the spectrum, the shape of the eye can widen fearfully. There will be notable tension around the eyes and in the brow. The fearful/anxious dog will look away from or glance sideways at the source of his problems. The pupils may dilate considerably if the dog is really stressed or becomes panicked. This change is due to shifts internally that result from the cascade of stress hormones that prepare a dog for flight/fight.

The worried dog who wants to signal apology ("I am sorry!") or appeasement ("Please don't be so angry/scary/threatening to me!") will have a partially closed eye that may be accompanied by a wrinkled brow. This is usually accompanied by other changes in the body language that says the dog is not seeking any confrontation.

The annoyed or irritated dog has eyes that flatten slightly, just as you would see in an annoyed person. This can be brief or sustained. Exactly how irritable or annoyed the dog is can be determined from other body language details.

Changes in lips

Lips are so expressive! Get a feel for how the dog normally looks when relaxed, particularly how he holds his mouth and lips (also known as the *commissure*). Are the lips held tightly? drawn back? panting? drawn forward?

Tension around the lips and muzzle indicate a problem. The more fearful/anxious the dog is, the more drawn back the lips become. The more fear that is involved, the tighter the lips become. An anxious dog may be panting with a wide, open mouth, and lips drawn way back. A fearful/anxious dog can also snarl, exposing the teeth in a threat intended to make a person or another dog stop and go away.

When a dog is becoming annoyed or angry, the lips may tighten and the corners are drawn forward. As the dog's annoyance or anger increases, you will begin to see a "rumpling" of the whisker bed, giving the dog's muzzle a lumpy look. This rumpling precedes an actual snarl which is meant to partially or completely expose the teeth as a threat.

Changes in whiskers

Learn to recognize what is normal for your dog in terms of how he holds his whiskers when relaxed and at other times. This can be difficult to see in the heavily bearded dogs, as the whiskers are hidden in thick coat. In show dogs who have had these important sensory devices removed, the missing whiskers cannot offer any useful clues.

A stressed dog (fearful, confused, overwhelmed) often folds the whiskers and holds them back against the muzzle. This differs from the typical relaxed position where the whiskers are held at about a 45-degree angle from the muzzle.

A dog who is angry or challenging may have whiskers brought forward. A curious, relaxed dog will bring his whiskers very far forward as he investigates something new. Sometimes, the whiskers will come so far forward that the longest will go well past the tip of the nose!

Changes in head and eye movements

A relaxed, comfortable dog has slow, easy movements of the head and eyes. Watch dogs just hanging out, with nothing particular of interest going on, and you'll see small, smooth movements. Crinkle a plastic bag in your pocket, and watch what happens to the head and eye movements; they become sharper, quicker.

As dogs become more fearful, or even panicked, the head and eye movements can change to quick, darting movements. This may rapidly escalate to a complete freeze of all movements if the dog becomes deeply afraid and has no escape. This stillness will include the head and eyes turned slightly or markedly *away* from what concerns the dog.

On the other end of the scale, the dog who becomes very still and stares at something with ears up and fixed (think "locked on target") is heading up the scale towards possible aggression, with the whole body held quite still but oriented *towards* the target. This could also be predatory behavior, as you might see in a dog hoping you will throw his squeaky toy (prey) or eyeing the squirrel at the bird feeder.

Less dramatic but still important shifts in head and eyes occur when the dog looks away or turns head away from a person or other dog; this dog is actively avoiding confrontation. The message is: "I don't want any trouble here, please go away."

The "whale eye" refers to seeing the white of the eye. While it is normal in humans, it is not typical in dogs. This increased visibility of the sclera or white of the eye is due to the gaze being directed in one direction, and the head being oriented in a slightly different direction. This is similar to what happens when someone looks at you from "the corner of their eye"; they may be facing straight ahead but their eyes roll to the side to watch you. When combined with tension throughout the face, muzzle, and body, and altered breathing, the whale eye can be a serious warning from the dog that should be heeded.

Increase in muscular tension

As the dog's emotional state shifts, so will the overall tension in his body. Do not mistake stillness for "okay." Sometimes, a dramatic shift can be seen in the dog's feet—look for clenching of toes, a sign often seen as the dog's fear/anxiety increases. Dogs who are confident and challenging, or who are becoming annoyed or angry move up on their toes, whereas fearful dogs often clench or spread their toes before moving away (if they can). Of course, pay close attention to the degree of muscular tension throughout the dog's body. Increasing tension points to a problem.

Freezing

An overwhelmed dog may literally freeze, showing no movement. This is often seen in combination with the overall body posture pulled back and down and/or away from the perceived threat. Freezing should be taken very seriously. A dog who is in freeze may explode without any further warning into fight or flight if pushed further. The explosion can be both dramatic and damaging.

Do not mistake a frozen dog for one who is gladly accepting whatever is happening. Ignoring or misunderstanding the freeze is a common mistake and often at the heart of painful reports. "He just exploded with no warning."

A dog who is *accepting* of and not upset by whatever is happening continues to have normal movement of the body, head, and eyes, with no shifts in breathing.

A dog who is *enjoying* an event or interaction continues to demonstrate body language that says he is not feeling threatened or upset in any way. The tail may be softly wagging, the dog may be "smiling" with soft, relaxed mouth, and lolling tongue.

A dog who is simply *enduring* an unwelcome, alarming, painful, scary, or unpleasant event often freezes when he cannot escape. The internal pressure continues to build second by second. Should that internal pressure reach an intolerable level, the dog may explode in dramatic behavior.

An Act of Love

Understanding some of the ways in which dogs demonstrate shifts in their mental and emotional states of mind helps prevent misunderstanding. Additionally, when dogs see that you recognize the smaller shifts and respond appropriately, their trust in you can grow rapidly. This is not any different from you learning to trust someone who is very sensitive to any shifts in your behavior. When you know they see and react appropriately to even your most subtle signals, your trust can grow. It would be more difficult for you to trust someone who means well but simply cannot see the changes or respond appropriately.

When people say of someone, "Oh, he's so good with animals; they just love him and trust him almost immediately," you know that is a person who reads animals well and responds to them in ways that lets them know they are truly seen, heard and understood. Really seeing someone else, human or animal, is a sacred act of love and respect.

CHAPTER FOUR

Dog is in the Details

Details, not labels, tell the tale

One trainer wrote: "A dog who puts its feet on you, a dog who seems to like pinning you down in your chair with its head on your lap, is not being affectionate but rather treating you like a member of the pack that can be pushed, stepped on, and held down. Many veterinary behaviorists and trainers warn that such signs should be read for what they are. Dominance aggression in an overt form should come as no sudden surprise if this kind of behavior has been observed in the past."

It is unfortunate that this sweeping condemnation of dogs seeking contact is fairly often heard. Missing here are the details, because details make a difference. Not all nose nudges, head in lap, climbing on you, sleeping on your pillow, etc., means dominance. But how do you know the difference?

This is one of the big problems with labels. They are sloppy "big bucket" interpretations. Labels are not an accurate recounting of observed behaviors, and labels never faithfully describe the nuances, context, and interactions inherent in any behavior.

In my seminars, I pose this question. "A woman is running to-wards you screaming—is this good or bad?"

Reflexively, many in the audience answer, "Not good!" especial-ly the men, for some odd reason. I point out it's just your grandmother who is delighted that you've finally arrived for an overdue visit.

"A woman is running towards you screaming, and she has a knife! Is this good or bad?"

Again, the reflexive answer is, "Bad!" I point out it's the same grandmother who happened to be chopping vegetables for your favorite soup when she heard you had arrived and dashed from the kitchen with knife in hand.

Generally speaking, I don't care what position a dog is in until I also know the specifics of the body language. In the case of our screaming woman, the details would let me know that she was screaming with delight, not homicidal intent. Details of how she held and wielded the knife would give me further clues that she was unaware she still had the knife, while someone coming at me with an intent to use the knife would look quite different.

I once had a mature German Shepherd perched on my head and shoulders. Was he dominating me? Hardly! He had been knocked over by a wave at the beach, and, in his panicked re-sponse to being knocked off his feet, he climbed the only available safe place—me! Anyone observing the dog's body language would have known there was nothing aggressive or challenging in his be-havior. He was afraid, nothing more.

We know this in our human/human interactions. A simple bit of eye contact with someone can be inviting, challenging, flirting, warning, threatening, etc. None of this would be accurately de-scribed by the broad, vague label of "he made eye contact with me." Take a moment to think about the multitude of other signals that could accompany making eye contact. If someone were flirt-ing with you, what else might they be doing? If someone were threatening you, what might you see in their body language in addition to the eye contact? How is that different from friendly eye contact?

People often misread or misunderstand dog language, relying instead on a crude understanding of basic postures ("the dog was leaning on me") and categorizing them as bad or okay without any sensitivity to the gorgeous complexities of how dogs convey in precise detail what they are trying to say.

Tell me the dog leans on you. Tell me he leans with ears laid softly back, soft eyes, normal blink rate, normal breathing, little muscle tension, relaxed lips, curves in his body/head/neck, flexion of his joints, and a slow wagging tail, and I'll tell you: it's all good.

Tell me the dog leans on you with a slow or absent blink rate, with muscle tension throughout, with altered breathing, no active flexion in his joints, a stiff tail without a wag, and then I'll say there is a problem brewing.

A dog could be plastered on top of you while you're lying on the floor and be absolutely 100% friendly and affectionate (ask me about my German Shepherd shaped blankets!). Or you could be in very big trouble. But the gross posture is not the whole picture; the complete, detailed picture is what's important if you want to know what's going on with that dog.

One sweet dog sticks out in my mind as one who almost met her end when a trainer diagnosed her as unpredictably aggressive and dangerous, and recommended euthanasia. Understandably upset with this answer, though aware she had a problem, the handler made her way to me. As she was telling the story of how the dog had bitten her in the face without any provocation, this part of the story caught my attention: "She seemed fine with being petted, and then she flipped over and asked for a belly rub. I rubbed her belly for a while, but then she got stiff and just went nuts and bit me in the face."

I'd been watching this dog carefully as the handler and I talked. Over and over again, I saw the dog approach the handler, make brief contact and then move away. If the handler continued to pet her, the dog would stop moving, stand very still, hold her breath, and stop all movement in her eyes. When the handler lifted her hand, the dog would slide away out of reach.

I asked the handler to pet the dog for just three seconds and then take her hand away. In this fashion, she could give the dog a chance to say, "Thanks, that's enough," and move away, or to make it clear by leaning or nudging or a look back towards the handler that the petting could continue. She was surprised to see the dog accept the touch but then move away given the chance.

I then carefully coached her to notice what happened if she kept petting the dog past three seconds. The mouth closed, the breathing shifted, the eyes stopped moving, and the entire body became still. I had her remove her hand and watch the differences unfold. The dog's eyes relaxed, her body softened, she took a breath, and her mouth loosened as she stepped away.

This was a sensitive dog, cautious and not very confident. She sent clear signals about her state of mind, but her handler had not been able to read them correctly.

The handler confirmed that the biting incident had begun with her just petting the dog. Thinking that the dog enjoyed this as much as she did, the handler had persisted in the contact, even when the dog grew still and held her breath. The dog's next move was to slide into a belly-up position in an attempt to nicely bring the interaction to a halt. The dog was now belly up, quite still, with her tail and legs tucked against her body. The dog's head and neck was extended and turned away from the handler, with no eye contact. Far from asking for a belly rub, the dog's body language indicated, "Please stop!"

This was a dog who was feeling increasingly overwhelmed, and whose signals were being (accidentally) ignored. Pushed past her ability to cope, the dog bit. As dogs often do, she made contact with the closest body part—her handler's face. (This is very different from a dog who deliberately launches with intent at the upper torso, throat, or face.)

A relaxed dog asking for further, more intimate contact like a belly rub would have loose, relaxed limbs, curves through the body, regular rhythmic breathing. A relaxed tail, soft facial expression, and a loose mouth (if not actually open with the tongue lolling out!) would be typical of a dog enjoying a belly rub.

Fortunately for this dog, her handler learned how to read the details of her dog's body language, which changed their relationship in profound ways. This little rescue dog found someone she could trust to really understand what she was saying, and her need to bite to make her message heard disappeared.

Missing Details

I'm disturbed and puzzled by some of the scales used for determining aggression by many professionals, veterinary behaviorists, and researchers. At best, some of these scales are rather coarsely grained, with all nuance or detail absent. For example, this is taken from Dr. Karen Overall's aggression assessment form:

NR=no reaction
SL=snarl/lift lip
BG=bark/growl
SB=snap/bite

What I find incredible is that in the absence of a snarl/lip lift (the first level response noted), bark/growl, or snap/bite, **the dog is rated as not aggressive!** I am dismayed that top researchers appear to be content with this rather coarse scale, instead of more accurately ranking the very specific behaviors that long precede a growl, snarl, or snap. Long before a snarl/lip lift or growl, a dog may become still, hold his breath, stiffen, and offer other clear early warning. Push past that clear warning, and, yes, you'll probably encounter a snarl, growl, lip lift, or worse.

As trainers, we are people who deliberately journey into the territory known as Dog. Unlike casual tourists, I feel we have an obligation to become fluent in the native language, lest we misunderstand and, without meaning to, respond inappropriately to those we seek to understand. To become fluent requires that we see—really *see*—the dog before us.

They say God is in the details.

So is Dog.

CHAPTER FIVE

Connection & Control

If you're hanging onto your dog's body, it's because you've lost his mind!

Control is not always about connection, but connection is what makes control possible.

Connection is about two minds working together. If the connection is not there between you and your dog, you will be unable to direct him, help him, or really train him.

Connection can come and go. It takes time and practice to create a steady state of connection. Typically—and especially for adolescent dogs and the average human—the connection changes in quality, sometimes minute by minute. Your dog may be nicely tuned in to you, but you become distracted by your cell phone or a text or your own thoughts, and you tune your dog out. Or you may be very aware of your dog, but he's forgotten about you because he saw a squirrel or smelled something wonderful.

Learning to stay connected is an important goal when working with any dog, particularly adolescents or dogs with behavior problems. Think of it as a balancing act that requires constant adjustment and awareness. It's a lot like driving in traffic. You need to keep assessing and altering your responses based on what's happening around you in order to prevent an accident. When driving on a very quiet road with few or no other cars around, you can relax and be less vigilant—but you still have to practice good driving.

Sometimes, we get careless because we don't feel the need for deeply attentive driving. The same is true for you and your dog. Even in quiet settings, practice quality connection. It will pay off in big ways when things get more interesting or in more challenging situations. What is practiced becomes strong, and what is practiced with a focus on quality becomes powerful.

The quality of the skill matters deeply. A master builder takes the time to focus on the quality of the construction of a house, giving even the smallest or hidden details the same diligent attention that he gives to bigger, more obvious aspects such as window placement or roofing materials. In fact, one hallmark of a master craftsman is the attention to details that others may not even notice or appreciate, fine points that may even be hidden from view yet serve as the foundation on which much rests.

Building a strong, reliable connection with a dog requires diligence and attention to the details and to the quality. If your goal is to aim for the highest quality connection that is possible in that moment between you and your dog, then you have the foundation for all else.

When you choose for quality and mindfulness in even the smallest ways in your relationship with your dog, something splendid begins to happen. There is a cumulative effect of so many quality moments. One moment of connection builds on another and then another, and like snowflakes, they accumulate without effort or strain and yet in the end, something quite impressive is possible.

Handlers can find themselves puzzled by the distance betwen their longing for a strong connection, and the reality of what happens in this or that situation. More than a few handlers have earnestly told me, "But when we're alone at home, he's not like this! He's wonderful and we get on so well. Then I take him out of the house to enjoy a walk and *this* happens!"

This is usually a dog doing anything but appear connected to his handler. Sometimes, I could actually tell a passerby that the handler had just found the dog wandering on the road and was holding him till animal control arrived, and the passerby would believe us.

By contrast, one group I worked with was given an unfamiliar dog and the task of getting to know that dog in five minutes. They understood how to truly connect with the dogs through a rapid exploration of my Elemental Questions, and putting the answers to work so that each handler and dog was quickly working cooperatively. How well it worked was apparent when a visitor from corporate headquarters arrived, and after watching the group for a few minutes, told me, "I didn't know that the employees were allowed to bring their own dogs to work." What she observed between the handlers and dogs seemed to reflect relationships built in years of relationship, but what she was really seeing were high quality connections.

One clue that the connection may need work is dependence on equipment. If you need equipment to maintain control of your dog, understand you're hanging on to your dog's body because you've lost his mind! Sometimes, equipment is necessary, because the connection and the dog's skills (or yours) are not strong enough for that moment's challenges. That's okay! Just recognize that training is a process and keep aiming for the highest quality connection you can have in any moment.

When you make staying connected the goal of being with your dog in any situation, training equipment becomes secondary, a way to keep the dog safe, a way to send signals *in addition to your verbal and non-verbal signals.*

Many dogs are well-connected to their owners, right until something more interesting shows up! While this may be understandable, it can cause problems if you don't work to resolve it. Your dog needs to understand what I call **"Even though..."** training. This is covered in detail in Chapter Seven, but, quickly explained, it is a principle that says, "Even though X is happening, the dog still needs to remain connected to you."

Of course, that "Even though . . ." rule applies to handlers, too. The quality of connection is a choice that handlers make each time they allow themselves to go through the motions, each time they choose to mindfully practice connection with their dogs. This is not the dog's responsibility. It is the handler who must take responsibility for creating the degree of quality that is desired.

When connection is present, control becomes much easier. Trying to control a dog who is not connected to you serves no one, and can undermine the relationship. Everyone ends up feeling frustrated. When connection is at the heart of all you do, that is a wonderful place from which to spring.

CHAPTER SIX

Permission, Not Permissive

Hyperactive! Out of control! ADD! Reactive! Lacking self control!

These labels and many more are readily applied to so many dogs. What I often see is a dog who is confused, frustrated, lacking clear information, and left hanging out to dry by the handler. When handler-driven issues are properly addressed, these meaningless labels evaporate, and a cooperative, intelligent dog who can be successful is revealed. Yet the handler often isn't considered part of the dynamic that contributes to a dog's behavior.

Relationship Centered Training (RCT) always considers the relationship and how dog and human interact to create behavior. The human end of the leash sometimes contributes to unwanted behavior without intending to do so. Recognizing how that happens is key to resolving problems.

Something I see over and over again is handlers who often silently permit the dog to do as he pleases. No clear signals to the dog, no yes, no, or maybe so. Just tacit agreement with whatever the dog is doing.

Handlers may have quite a dialogue in their heads going on at any given moment:

"Oh, he just loves his friend Buster. I'm so glad he has doggie friends. No wonder he was pulling so hard; he saw his friend!"

"She was so abused and shy, I am just tickled that she's pulling me over to meet new people!"

"I know he gets so excited when he sees sheep, squirrels, cats, hedgehogs, balloons, water, toys, *[fill in your choice]*, I just can't control him!"

You know what dogs hears from handlers who are busy justifying and rationalizing their behavior? Nothing. What the dog believes is what the handler's actions tell him. This is the rule that guides his behavior.

You know what the dog may believe?

"If I see my friend Buster, I can drag my handler over there. She does move kind of slow, and she pulls too."

"I can go greet anyone I like. My handler isn't a part of this."

"I don't need to pay attention to my handler when there are more interesting things to see, do, or chase."

Many handlers are surprised when they stop to think about what their dog may believe the rules are. It's usually not what the handler had in mind at all.

To discover whether you may be permissive rather than someone who gives permission to the dog to do X, Y or Z, try my Silent Movie Experiment.

Videotape yourself training or just walking with your dog. Show this to a friend, and ask for a description of what you are working on in that video. Ask what the rules are for your dog's behavior based on that video. You may be surprised at what you hear.

Like silent movie audiences, dogs must guess from the action, not the words, what's happening and what is intended. Sometimes, handlers make very confusing movies.

When permission is *implicit*—meaning, it's not actually stated—the dog can understandably become confused. Worse, the dog may end up thinking he can do what he likes without needing to check with you.

Explicit permission involves deliberate signals that the dog can hear, feel, and see. These signals may be verbal cues, visual cues, even touch cues. The signals may also be your entire body language and actions. For example, when I say, "Go say hi," I drop my head briefly, extend an arm or hand towards the person/animal to be greeted, and step towards them along with my dog. This makes my message explicit and crystal clear to the dog.

This is very different from the full body message of "no, sorry, not now" that I may give in another situation. In that case, I would stand still, look towards the person/animal but then back at the dog, with a small head shake and perhaps a small gesture that means "stay here with me." The dog is not confused. He knows I recognize the situation but have made a decision and provided him with direction.

When you give explicit permission, you gain a great deal:
- clarity for both you and the dog about what is intended and permitted
- control over behavior, especially behavior driven by strong motivations

Explicit permission is useful information about YES and NO. If you can say, for example, "Go say hi!" at times, you can also say "not now" at others. This allows the dog to understand clearly that there are times when behavior X is fine, but times when it is not.

Avoid those conversations that take place only in your head. Your dog will be grateful for the clarity of shared information. Explicit permissions are not just good training; they are courteous conversations.

CHAPTER SEVEN

"Even though. . ."

A simple rule that builds powerful relationships

All of us can appreciate what might excite a dog, even to the point of tuning out his handler. It could be another dog, people approaching, food, toys, wildlife, a cat or squirrel, anticipation of a happy event like a walk, or being in class. We understand that the world is full of many things our dogs may find far more interesting than a conversation with us.

Handlers often excuse their dog's excitability. "Oh, he just gets so excited when he sees another dog, he just has to go right over and say hi!" or "He just loves coming to class, and he's so friendly I can't control him!" or "Whenever he sees a squirrel, he just loses his mind!" When handlers say such things, I know two things are probably true:

1. The handler understands these triggers for excited or out of control behavior.
2. The handler is probably confusing the dog.

It is good that the handler understands the dog's motivation. It is not good if that empathy with the dog's feelings leads to allowing the dog to act rudely. Do be empathetic to your dog's needs and desires. But, be cautious as to how you let that empathy create unclear expectations for your dog. He may learn that if he's excited about seeing a dog, he will be allowed to pull you right over for a meeting.

Often, the dog ends up being blamed for not having self-control when, in fact, the handler has taught him it's okay to pull and tune her out. More often than not, it is the handler who needs to have and maintain clear rules, and learn how to provide explicit permission signals.

You can help a confused dog by creating clarity in your expectations. My **"Even though..."** approach teaches the dog that despite whatever is going on around him, his job is to remain connected to you.

> *Even though a cat just entered the room, stay connected to me.*
>
> *Even though you see your best doggy pal, stay connected to me.*
>
> *Even though that nice lady has treats in her pocket...*
>
> *Even though that guy just threw a ball for his dog...*
>
> *Even though we're headed for the training class...*

It is amazing how fast dogs who have been labeled as "lacking self-control" calm right down and become cooperative when the handler can set clear expectations. Practice "Even though..." training and connection everywhere and reap the rewards.

"Even though..." applies equally to humans and dogs. Some common moments where handlers may need to take care to stay connected to their dogs:

> *Even though my cell phone just rang...*
>
> *Even though my friend is chatting with me...*
>
> *Even though I have a lot on my To-Do list . . .*
>
> *Even though I'm worried about my job/taxes/hair...*

Combined with explicit permission, the "Even though…" principle helps your dog understand that, while you recognize his needs, he needs to wait for permission from you before he acts on what he sees or hopes for or wants to do.

Be with your dog, even though…, and you can expect the same from him. It's the stuff quality relationships are made of—try it.

CHAPTER EIGHT

Hard to Train?

A look at "difficult-to-train" breeds
and the reality of what shapes these canine minds

Imagine two balloons hanging over your dog's head. One balloon asks, "Why?" *Why should I heel/stay/come/retrieve/jump?* The other asks, "Why not?" *Why not chew the shoe, walk over here, eat your sandwich?*

I believe that these two questions (and the answers received) are among the primary inquiries that shape a dog's relationship with his humans. To the extent that we are able to provide satisfactory answers to these simple questions, an extraordinary amount of information can be communicated between ourselves and our dogs. But there is, inevitably, a catch. The answers that we think are satisfactory may fail to satisfy the dog. And, being a dog, he turns away and gets on with his life while we fumble for more appropriate responses.

In a deliciously ironic twist, our deliberate selection for certain behavioral traits in purebred dogs has led to the development of breeds who, some more strenuously than others, insist on interesting, well-thought-out answers to the two primary life questions.

For example, a Border Collie might ask, "Why?" and be perfectly satisfied with an answer of "Because I told you to." Driven by a desire to work—even if it's busy work—a Border Collie questions no further. On the other hand, a Siberian Husky receiving such an answer might simply cock his head and gaze at his handler with barely contained amusement. (Every Siberian worth his salt knows that "Because I told you to" is not an acceptable answer.) And the dialogue begins.

> Handler: You should do this because you love me.
> Siberian *(truthfully):* Love is a feeling, not a reason.
> Handler *(a bit pompous):* It is important that you do this.
> Siberian *(with great wisdom):* Humans give importance to the wrong things.
> Handler *(growing angry):* If you don't do this, I'll punish you.
> Siberian *(with dignity):* Then I may have no choice but to comply. But, I can choose not to trust or like you.
> Handler *(calmer, trying another approach):* I'll make it fun for you.
> Siberian *(interested):* How much fun?
> Handler: So much fun that you'll beg for more!
> Siberian: On that basis, I'll try it. But remember, I'm easily bored. This better be good.

Now, if the handler was trying to get this Siberian to run, the dialogue would be much different:

> Handler: I want you to run like the wind.
> Siberian: I'm already gone!

Why?

At one of my seminars, a handler presented her dog with this complaint: "She just won't stop sniffing the ground while we're heeling, and I'm tired of being embarrassed in the obedience ring.

I just don't understand why she does this. What can I do to stop her from sniffing?"

Looking down at her dog, I had a hard time not laughing. It was a Bloodhound, behaving precisely as generations of selective breeding insisted that she behave. When I asked why she was so determined to put advanced obedience titles on this dog, the handler responded, "Well, very few Bloodhounds do well in obedience. So, I'm going to do it with this dog."

Technically speaking, all of the obedience exercises were within the dog's physical and mental abilities. The trick, of course, was in the training approach. Whatever the approach being used, it obviously failed to answer the dog's very legitimate question of "Why?" (Or, perhaps more accurately in this case, "Why not sniff?") And until the handler came up with a better answer, the dog was going to continue doing what she enjoyed doing and had been bred to do—sniff the ground.

Here's a basic formula for one cause of training problems:

The greater the distance X is from Z,
the more you will have to explain Y.
X = Desired behavior
Z = Genetically programmed behavior
Y = WHY?

In other words, it's not difficult to get a retriever to retrieve, a herding dog to herd, or a Siberian to run. But, you better have some pretty good answers when you send a Mastiff or a Greyhound out to retrieve a duck in icy waters.

Easy to train?

There are three basic qualities that make a dog "easy to train."

- Intelligence (which I define as the dog's awareness of and curiosity about his world)
- Willingness (the dog's desire to interact with other beings)
- Confidence (physically, emotionally and intellectually)

Now, to be sure, a good many of the "difficult to train" breeds possess these qualities in generous measure. Add in the considerable athletic ability of many "difficult" breeds, and you have, in theory, a dog who can learn to do almost anything. Of course, the less a dog possesses of these three basic qualities, the more difficult it becomes to adequately answer "Why?" and "Why not?" The dull-witted, shy/timid, or highly independent dog simply may not care much about your answers.

There are three other qualities which impact on training.

- Sense of humor (what dogs find tremendously funny does not always tickle the human on the other end of the lead)
- Boredom threshold (which are often much lower than humans imagine)
- Selectively bred behaviors (which are not always in alignment with human behaviors or in keeping with our training goals—*thus the Bloodhound in the obedience ring!*)

Each breed is a unique blend of these six characteristics in varying proportions.

The "easy to train" breeds are characterized by high boredom thresholds; they are willing to repeat even relatively meaningless tasks for long periods. They also possess a range of selectively bred behaviors that are either very broadly applicable or particularly well-suited to the common tasks of the obedience or agility ring.

The supposedly "tough" breeds, characterized by low boredom thresholds, quickly grow bored with repetitions and/or activities they find pointless. They also possess a fairly narrow spectrum of selectively bred behaviors and are best suited to highly specialized tasks. Those who are successful with "tough" breeds are creative handlers willing and able to make training fun, interesting, and relevant to the dog. They can answer "Why?" and "Why not?" with great clarity, humor, and respect for what makes that breed unique.

Know the Individual Dog

As with any breed, successful training of the "difficult" breeds begins with a relationship of mutual trust and affection. There is also a degree of intimacy involved. You must know the dog for who he is. Not what you hope he will become, but who he is at any given moment in your journey together. What amuses him? Does he like exuberant praise or games or treats? What does he consider a reward? What worries him? Delights him? How does he learn? In intuitive leaps or seamless progression? Or in small chunks that he struggles to master? Whether Siberian or Schnauzer, there is no single recipe for training success except this— intimate knowledge of the individual dog and yourself.

In our pack of seven dogs, we have seven vastly different minds. For example, my husband's Golden, Molson, is willing to work hard, even if the handler's mind is not totally on the training process. But, teaching her new tricks is difficult. She believes, for reasons we cannot fathom, that each successfully mastered step is the whole trick, and is momentarily frustrated when we ask for a bit more, like a slightly higher or longer wave of her paw. So, we train slowly, in small chunks, and often intersperse her old tricks to offer her some relief. "This I know how to do!" Food is a powerful motivator for this dog.

In contrast, Grizzly, our youngest German Shepherd, makes intuitive leaps, is highly creative, and often generalizes his knowledge to fit new situations. He is not easily frustrated, but he requires that we are as enthusiastic and focused as he is. Half-hearted training gets half-hearted responses from Grizzly. While motivated by food, he loves to retrieve and roughhouse; so, games with toys and sessions of tug are powerful rewards for him.

Asking Questions is a Smart Dog's Job

In a world of trainers who often prefer dogs who don't ask many questions, where "good dogs" are the dogs who bend easily to the control and demands of rather arbitrary rules and regulations, there are far too many breeds who have a reputation of being stubborn, tough to train, and willful. What this often means is that this "difficult dog" is an intelligent dog who asks too many questions for the average trainer. Such a canine mind is not automatically compliant and comes equipped with its own view of the

world and its own definitions of what constitutes meaningful, enjoyable activities. This is not to say these dogs are not willing—one
of the great charms of these breeds is their keen interest in life and
in people. If given the right answers to "Why?" and "Why not?"
many of these dogs can be not just agreeable but downright bril-
liant in the execution of a task.

There are breeds who "carry" their handlers, politely ignoring
human failings while carrying out the assigned task with style. By
and large, the "difficult breed" dog comes just halfway, standing
his ground in confidence, with a glint of humor in his eye, waiting
for the handler to match him stride for stride. Seeking precision?
Then you, these dogs often insist, must also be precise. Fun on
your terms? Then you must also learn to have fun on the dog's
terms. Is it enthusiasm you seek? Then, you must not only find a
way to make learning and performing enjoyable, you must also
give yourself 100% to the task. The "tough to train" dog works
well in a team, but he will only pull his share of the load.

CHAPTER NINE

Guidelines for Teaching Self-Control

Teach your dog self-control as the foundation for all other learning

Does your dog pull on the lead when someone approaches? When he sees another dog? What if joggers run by? If children are playing? If a cat or squirrel dashes through the yard? Is he hard to control at the vet's or groomer's? When people come into your house?

If the answer to any of these questions is yes, chances are good that, among other skills, your dog needs to learn self-control. Just as children must learn to control their impulses before they can mature into responsible adults, dogs must learn self-control before they can become well-mannered canine citizens. Self-control is a specific skill that must be taught, just as you teach your dog to sit or speak or come when called.

In teaching self-control, the handler needs to be aware of how their own behavior, choices of equipment, and methods can be supportive of the dog and developing self-control, or contributing to unwanted behavior.

Here is the picture of a handler using appropriate equipment and methods to help a dog learn self-control:

The handler is in control of herself and her emotions, with congruence between her thoughts, actions, body language, and gestures. As social animals, dogs will pay close attention to the model we offer in any given situation, so the handler needs to model thoughtful, aware, and appropriate behavior in each situation. Her voice is clear, with expression that modulates depending on what the dog needs to hear—praise? direction? support? reminders?

The training equipment is used to provide clear, gentle signals that give the dog information he needs to be successful. The handler does not use the training equipment to drag, pull, manipulate, or guide the dog, but instead, uses gestures and aware use of space to help the dog. The handler works constantly to eliminate any tension on the leash, recognizing that a dog exhibiting self-control is a dog who can hold himself in place on a loose leash; he is literally controlling himself without being restrained.

Self-control is practiced in many settings, always with the dog in the Think & Learn Zone™. As with any practice, the dog may need reminders. For example, you might ask the dog to lie quietly beside you for a few minutes. If the dog thinks about getting up, remind him quietly with another "down" cue (verbal, hand signal, or both).

His attention will wander and the exciting things in the environment may pull him out of position. Expect this and be ready to help him return to the practice and do this over and over. If it helps, see the dog as asking, "Do I still have to keep doing this?" Your actions should spell out an unwavering, "Yes, you do." There is no need to "correct" the dog, but there is a need to be relentless in the quiet insistence that he continue practicing until formally released.

Ideally, help the dog with a reminder, when he is thinking about moving, and offer low key praise for his resuming the right position. If the dog should move before you can help him, move calmly to him, and guide him back to precisely the spot where you want him.

Work in short, sweet sessions so that the dog can be successful. Ten three-minute sessions scattered across the day in various locations can do more good than one 30-minute session in one location. Self-control is a skill that is developed through practice; build that mental muscle through many repetitions but without overdoing it. Teach your dog self control by following these guidelines:

Learn how to determine whether your dog is in the Think & Learn Zone™. With a simple approach, you can ask your dog, "Can you think and learn here?" If he can, you can practice self-control exercises there, wherever it may be. If he can't, you'll need to adjust things until the answer is yes. (Details on this in Chapter Ten, *Understanding Thresholds.*)

Remember the dog does not know what his options are. A dog who is lacking self-control simply does not know that it is possible to sit or lie quietly in the face of distractions. It is the handler's responsibility to show the dog that he has options other than lunging, pulling, or leaping around.

Move slowly and talk quietly. A dog who is highly excited needs calm, slow handling. Common mistakes that handlers make include moving quickly, grabbing at the leash and collar, raising their voice, and speaking in short, sharp tones. From the dog's point of view, the handler appears as excited as he is, and short sharp tones often sound like barking. Instead of calming the dog, this reinforces the dog's excitement. By moving slowly and talking quietly, handlers send a clear message to the dog that they are not excited and are in control of the situation. Be the model for self-control in your own actions.

Remind and ask, don't demand. A dog who is already excited is likely to resist a harsh correction or respond by becoming more excited. "Ask" by using the lightest possible touch on the leash and collar, and remind the dog what he's doing each time he forgets and shifts position. Keep the leash loose except when sending a specific signal.

Ask for compliance, not submission. Work with your dog as you would with any friend. Avoid creating a struggle by asking the dog for more than he can do at the time. For example, if your dog is really excited, he may be unable or unwilling to lie down, but agreeable to sitting quietly with a few reminders from you. Conversely, some dogs find sitting uncomfortable and would prefer to lie down. Choose a position that is comfortable—being comfortable helps the dog to succeed. Compromise and be reasonable. Many struggles between dog and handler are created when the handler attempts to argue with or wrestle the dog, instead of finding a solution acceptable to both owner and dog.

Train, don't restrain. Taking a firm grip on the leash and collar teaches the dog nothing except that you can restrain him. Self-control is the dog holding *himself* under his own control, not an animal being physically held back. A loose leash tells the tale of self-control versus restraint.

Work on teaching self control in all situations. Begin by working in distraction-free areas and ask your dog to sit or lie down on a loose leash for no more than five minutes. Thirty seconds here, a minute there, three minutes there—it all adds up. Focus on the quality of each session (loose leash, able to control himself), not the quantity. Gradually, move on to more exciting situations, and practice often in brief sessions. Work at home, at friends' homes, in parks, shopping centers, at dog shows, training classes, and the veterinarian's. As your dog's self-control increases, you can add lying down quietly for up to 30 minutes to his skills.

CHAPTER TEN

Understanding Thresholds: It's More than Under or Over

What's too much? Too little? How do you know?

It is often heard and cheerfully given advice: "Keep him under threshold!" Yep. Can do. I think. Maybe. Um, how do I know?

Successfully negotiating any given situation requires the appropriate degree of arousal. The arousal level necessary to run an agility course is not the same as working on a paw trick in the kitchen. But whatever the situation, chances are very good that you want your dog in the sweet spot for optimum response and learning—what I call the Think & Learn Zone™.

The Think & Learn Zone is the state of arousal where your dog can still control himself, think and apply known skills, learn, be responsive to you, be socially appropriate, and make good decisions. Too much arousal and your dog's ability to be responsive, appropriate, or even think begins to shred or disappear altogether.

This is not a matter of speed or activity—a dog can be moving very fast and still in the Think & Learn Zone. (Good thing for agility handlers!) A dog can also be lying absolutely still and be far out of the Think & Learn Zone. Two key aspects distinguish the Think & Learn Zone: *splitting attention* and *responsiveness*.

When in the Think & Learn Zone, the dog can split his attention between the stimulus and his handler. If the dog's attention is focused solely on the stimulus, no training can be accomplished, and you may trigger unwanted behavior or reactions. If the dog's attention isn't on the stimulus, no reaction occurs—but neither does any learning about the stimulus. While certainly sub-threshold, it's also useless.

Being responsive is also a hallmark of the Think & Learn Zone. The dog can respond appropriately and *accurately* to the handler's direction, cues or signals, as well as to the environment and others around him. The dog who is offering what I call "sticky" responses or inaccurate responses is telling you that he is moving out of the Think & Learn Zone.

A dog who is not responsive has left the Think & Learn Zone, which means not much, if any, learning or thinking is occurring.

Finding the Think & Learn Zone

Whether over-stimulated or afraid or even seriously aggressive, the specifics of how to successfully work with reactive dogs is based on appropriate use of the *Stimulus Gradient*. Understanding the Stimulus Gradient (SG) helps handlers recognize an individual dog's thresholds and make good decisions in any situation.

Thoughtfully applied, the SG can make it much easier to keep a dog progressing without pushing him too hard. A dog who is over-threshold is out of the Think & Learn Zone, and no real learning occurs. The SG can also help handlers avoid spinning their wheels by working under-threshold, where no real learning occurs. The principles behind the SG can help a handler understand what went wrong if a mistake occurs—and know how to adjust for success.

Some definitions are helpful:

- **Stimulus:** *causes an action or response; also sometimes referred to as a trigger.* This could be as simple as a noise, another dog, birds, a cat, children running, a biker.
- **Gradient:** *gradual change across a range.* Sunrise and sunset are everyday examples of a gradient. The rising sun grows increasingly brighter; the setting sun, increasingly less bright.
- **Stimulus Gradient:** *refers to the increase or decrease of a stimulus.*

There are three elements to the Stimulus Gradient (SG): distance, duration, and intensity. Just as you adjust a stereo system by dialing the bass, treble, and balance up or down in relationship to each other, the SG allows you to adjust the elements of distance, intensity, and duration with any given stimulus in order to help your dog think, learn, and succeed.

Distance (or Proximity)

Distance refers to how far away the dog is from the stimulus. The further away, the less provoking the stimulus will be. You might be afraid of spiders, but you're probably not bothered by spiders in the Amazon. Somewhere between the jungles of Brazil and your current position lies the point at which you begin to feel uneasy, and it's at a point when the spider is closer to you.

There is no one good or right distance; it always depends on the dog, the specific stimulus, and the specific situation. Many times, handlers report with some surprise, "Well, I don't know why he reacted so badly. That other dog/person/cat/jogger was more than 25 feet away!" as if, somehow, at 25 feet, a stimulus should lose its power to affect the dog.

The only distance at which dogs can be assumed to be okay with a given stimulus is the distance that puts the stimulus out of the dog's perceptual range. The dog cannot react to a stimulus that he cannot hear, smell, feel, see, or touch.

I've worked with dogs who reacted intensely to a stimulus that was hundreds of feet away, dogs who only reacted when the stimulus was within inches, and dogs who reacted when they could only smell the stimulus. I've worked with dogs who were so precise that a change of just an inch or two was enough to change the situation from acceptable to not acceptable. The dog is the only one who can determine what distance is suitable for him.

When you get within 25 feet or so, begin to consider distances in terms of the dog's body length, not in foot measurements. As humans, we tend to report distances in very human terms, since we are not significantly different from each in size. Dogs, on the other hand, fit on a broad spectrum of sizes. Being 10 feet away from a Saint Bernard may only represent three body lengths for him, but it might be 10 body lengths for the Manchester Terrier. The Saint allowing someone to roll past on a skateboard three body lengths away will look very different from the Manchester also allowing the skateboard three body lengths. Think of distance relative to the individual dog.

Be precise in using and marking the distance so that you can track how any change in distance affects the dog. Dogs are particularly sensitive to distance, and surprisingly small changes can give you very different responses. Use natural markers in the environment, if necessary. In a training room or arena, try using bits of tape or yarn on fencing, or taped out marks on the floor or walls to give all people involved a clear sense of distances.

Distance can be altered by bringing the dog closer to the stimulus, or by bringing the stimulus closer to the dog. Each has its advantages, depending on what you are trying to achieve. Be aware that another dog, a person, or other animal coming closer to the dog not only closes the distances but also creates social pressure which may add to the intensity.

Duration

Duration is a measurement of time. How long will the dog be asked to deal with the stimulus? Will it appear only briefly, or be there for three minutes or 30 minutes, an hour or all day?

Have a specific time frame in your mind. For example, *I will present stimulus X for a count of 1-2-3, and then remove it.* Avoid casual time frames, such as "Let's try that for a while," or "That's probably enough." Increasing or decreasing "a while" or "enough" usually doesn't prove helpful to the dog.

Measuring duration helps you decide how to be most helpful to the dog when it is necessary to increase or decrease the duration. The dog might be successful with a duration of 18 seconds but, by 20 seconds, not be able to handle the stimulus. Knowing this, you might opt to spend more time working on a 15-second duration of stimulus to help the dog succeed before trying to increase the duration further.

How long will you expose the dog to the stimulus? A good rule of thumb is *not long!* Ideal duration depends heavily on distance and intensity. It might be only *seconds*. When in doubt, use brief duration exposures to the stimulus, and evaluate what the dog tells you. If the dog is slow to settle or completely loses his ability to be responsive to the handler, the duration (and/or intensity and/or distance) is too much.

Many trainers not only work too close, but expect far too much in the way of duration. The ideal duration is one that leaves the dog about as relaxed as he was *prior to the presentation of the stimulus.*

Intensity

How intense is the stimulus? Many factors affect intensity, including duration and distance, which must always be taken into account. Intensity can vary with the size, loudness, volume, strength, pressure, speed, movement, color, appearance, sex, smell, quality, or quantity of any given stimulus presented to the dog.

Simply put, one cat sitting quietly far away with his back to the dog is much lower intensity than 24 yowling cats practicing their *River Dance* routine in the living room.

One dog's sensory sensitivities can make something quite intense for him, while another dog might not find it as intense. Understand how the individual dog prioritizes sensory input and what affect it has on him. This will help you evaluate the intensity of any given stimulus for that individual dog. For example, a visually-sensitive dog might find a raised arm to be a very intense gesture, whereas a less visually-sensitive dog might not react until you run past him.

The orientation of the stimulus can alter its intensity significantly. A person sitting quietly facing away from the dog is less intense than the same person sitting quietly facing the dog. Even a stuffed animal, statue, or garden gnome becomes less intense if facing away from the dog.

The speed, quality, and magnitude of movement will also alter the intensity of the stimulus. Big gestures are typically more intense than smaller ones; smooth movements are less intense than quick, jerky movements. Something moving slowly past the dog is (usually) less intense than something moving past rapidly. But sometimes, a slow or cautious movement can be perceived by the dog as threatening or weird, and increase intensity. Quick movements can also be seen as threatening. Stillness itself can be threatening if combined with direct orientation and/or eye contact.

While adjusting distance or duration is fairly straightforward, adjusting intensity to make it just right for the dog can be challenging even for experienced trainers.

Basic Guidelines

The three elements of the Stimulus Gradient need to be juggled and adjusted with care and deliberate awareness of what effect any combination will have on the dog. When the balance is right, the dog is in the Think & Learn Zone, a setting where he can improve (sometimes rapidly).

- Always give the dog the benefit of the doubt.
- Always make the dog successful.
- When you change one element, lighten up the other two.
- Avoid saying, "Just one more time."
- End it while it's good and the dog is successful.
- Avoid waiting till the dog says he can't handle any more.

When unsure:
Increase Distance
and
Decrease Duration & Intensity

CHAPTER ELEVEN

Rewards, Lures and Bribes

Which is which?

In living with and working with dogs, rewards as well as bribes and lures have a distinct place and value at certain points in the training process. But what exactly is a reward, a bribe, or a lure? Knowing the difference can help you avoid the drawbacks and emphasize the value of each.

Lures

A lure (from the Latin for "to invite") is defined as "to tempt with a promise of pleasure or gain; implies a drawing into . . . through attracting and deceiving."

Depending on the dog's interests, a lure can be food, a toy, a leaf, stick, feather, empty hand, or tug—just about anything that can be effectively used by the handler.

A lure is offered *before* a behavior is elicited and either directly assists in guiding the behavior or minimizes/eliminates the stumbling blocks of confusion and uncertainty. In the simple act of following the lure, a dog can learn or see the path or posture that is wanted. Used properly, a lure helps smooth the way and makes learning easier. Once that mission is accomplished, the lure should be faded quickly.

Because lures help to make you and your actions of greater interest to the animal, a lure can be a quick way to establish a relationship and gain cooperation from animals you don't know well. A puppy might see no point in following your hand to the floor as you try to guide him to lie down. But, a tidbit can show him that you are more interesting than he thought.

Lures loan themselves beautifully to being faded into hand signals and gestures. The puppy who learns to sit because he follows a hand holding a tidbit can take the next step to quickly learning that the same hand gesture without a tidbit means SIT. Fade lures quickly once the dog has the concept to avoid creating a dog dependent on the treat or toy lure being present in order to perform the behavior.

However, a lure presented when a dog is quite anxious or actually afraid can significantly pressure a dog. A lure should never put a dog into conflict between wanting the lure and feeling anxious or afraid. When fear or anxiety is present to any notable degree, avoid using lures, and switch to using rewards for behaviors that the dog can perform successfully with a calm demeanor.

In the definition above, a lure works "through attracting and deceiving." Using lures to deceive the dog slides close to or right into bribe territory. This usually results in a dog who no longer trusts the human (rightfully so), and a human who proclaims, "Food rewards don't work!" There must be both honesty and integrity in the use of lures.

The most common error I see in the use of lures is the failure to fade the lure. This leads to a dog who refuses to cooperate unless lured; both handler and dog need to make the transition to rewards, not lures.

Bribes

A bribe is defined as something "that serves to induce or influence."

To my mind, the most important difference between a lure and a bribe is the intent behind the offer. A bribe is a deceitful attempt to gain or regain control, while a properly used lure is a more pure-hearted, genuine attempt to ease the way and make the learning of a lesson a little more pleasant.

A bribe is an offer made in an attempt to get a dog to do something he chooses not to. This offer most often occurs just prior to ("If you do that, you can have this") or concurrent with ("I'll make it worthwhile to comply") the cue.

I do use bribes—sparingly. This is **not** training; it is just management of a situation. Bribes can be an effective means of temporarily solving a particularly dangerous or frustrating situation. Once that is resolved, turn your attention to training what is really needed in that situation.

A dog who is delightedly charging around the house with a chicken carcass may not drop it on command, but may be quite willing to "trade it" for a bribe of cheese dramatically offered or a favorite toy. Teach the drop skill very thoroughly at some other, less critical moment; in the moment, use a bribe to solve the problem.

Staying out in the yard and playing "catch me if you can" is a frustrating game loved by dogs (especially adolescents) and loathed by owners. The solution is to teach a rocket fast recall in response to a signal. If the dog only rarely insists on wanting to stay out, I might just use a bribe, such as an unexpected shake of the treats can. If this is a more regular occurrence, I'd turn a bribe into both a signal and a reward by associating the noise of the treat can with an unfailing promise to have a cookie party for any dog who gets his butt in the house.

Bribes are the number one reason disgruntled handlers mutter about the folly of using food rewards. As you'll see in the next section, rewards are invaluable in training and work beautifully. Bribes are only temporary solutions; long term, they will backfire on you and your dog.

How do you recognize a dog who is accustomed to bribes and not true rewards? He has a bumper sticker that says, "First, show me the cookies."

Rewards

The dictionary definition of reward is "something that is given in return for good or evil done or received; and especially that is offered or given for some service..."

Rewards are also known as reinforcement, or positive reinforcement. A reward is always unexpected, unseen, and comes after the appropriate behavior or response. A reward is a consequence for a behavior, and a positive consequence at that.

A reward can be anything that the dog likes. There are many things and activities that a dog might consider a reward. You just have to take the time to observe the dog and find out what he enjoys, finds interesting, or seeks out on his own.

CHAPTER TWELVE

Using Consequences

Encourage, discourage, and do it all effectively & humanely

Here is one simple truth about training. We can either encourage or discourage behavior.

Can it be that easy? That seems far too simple. True, the animal training world is full of terminology and technicalities. Such technical knowledge can be useful, and it is fun learning the jargon. But knowing the jargon is not the same as knowing the dog.

For the sake of the dog, take all the terminology you know, and distill it to the essence of what you are really doing. That lets simple, powerful truths and the dog shine through.

We encourage or discourage by providing consequences, assuming we wish to change behavior. (If we don't want to change behavior, we do nothing; we're neutral.)

Consequences tell the dog: "*This* is what happens when you do *that*." When consequences are effective, they change the dog's behavior. So there you have it, training in a nutshell.

Encourage or discourage, and evaluate your effectiveness by the changes in behavior. Simple! But that's an awful lot like saying that successfully painting a landscape requires that you put the green where the green goes and the blue where the blue goes, and so on. That is true, but painting—like training—involves many careful considerations.

Yea or Nay?

Consequences can be positive or negative. Positive consequences are pleasurable for the dog. They are fun, enjoyable, delicious, pleasant, or in some way valuable to the dog. Positive consequences are usually called rewards or positive reinforcement.

Negative consequences are not pleasurable for the dog. When a behavior results in *negative consequences*, the dog is *discouraged* from doing that behavior again.

If the positive consequence is effective, you will see *more* of the behavior you want. If a negative consequence is effective, you will see *less* of the unwanted behavior.

Relationship Centered Training focuses on helping the dog learn which behaviors result in positive consequences. We want the dog to be *right* so that we can encourage and reward him—a lot! This is different from traditional dog training, which focuses on punishing or correcting unwanted behaviors.

RCT also chooses to lean heavily on positive consequences for the dog. As the old saying points out, "You can catch more flies with honey than vinegar." We dispense a lot of honey.

Always ask how you can use positive consequences to encourage a dog to do what you'd like him to do, instead of using negatives to discourage him. An encouraged dog keeps trying and has fun learning.

Accentuate the Positive

Positive consequences can be anything that the dog considers good. Here's a brief list of some of rewards I've used with various dogs: food treats, toys, touch, hunting for crickets, freedom to sniff, a feather, playing tug, taking off the leash, opening a door, getting into the car, a postcard, leaves, grass, a game of tag, and being squirted with water.

In each case, the specific dog found that specific reward meaningful, pleasant and worth receiving in exchange for his behavior(s). Had I used cricket hunting as a reward for the dog who enjoyed being squirted with a water gun, he might have been very puzzled, if not offended. The cricket hunter would have been quite upset to have me offer her a postcard. **Rewards are meaningful only if the dog says they are.**

Food treats can range from ho-hum "rice cake" type treats, such as dry kibble or biscuits, to "birthday cake!"—treats like meats, jerky, cheese, and other food items that are particularly appealing to a dog. Know what floats your dog's boat, and use it to send clear messages. A simple thank you can be conveyed with a small "rice cake" type treat. A huge thank you involves many "birthday cake" ones.

How you deliver that birthday cake party makes a world of difference. Don't just give the dog a handful of cookies; involve yourself in the delivery of every bit of the reward.

I love teaching handlers to deliver many teeny tiny treats, given one at a time with delight clear in your voice as you say short praise phrases like, "You are a genius! That was fantastic! Well done! Good work, buddy!" and so on. Each little phrase accompanies one more treat. You're smiling. You're looking into the dog's eyes. You're keeping up a rhythm of treat-praise phrase-treat-praise phrase-treat and so on at a speed that allows him to swallow and enjoy each treat, not choke on it. The smooth continued flow of treats helps the dog understand that this is all one big "You are awesome!" party.

This treat-praise phrase delivery also makes sure that the party goes on and on for a while. When you do that with 10–15 treats, that celebration goes on for at least 10 seconds, if not more. Most dogs have never had a 10-second celebration in their lives, and believe me, they remember that party. It makes a big impression. Plus, it's fun to really help a dog enjoy his reward by involving yourself. This is quite different from the disengaged approach of "Hey, look, I threw a bunch of treats over there. Good dog."

Generosity counts when using rewards, particularly if you're careful to reward efforts in the way they deserve. A well-trained behavior does not need a big party; a new behavior or breakthrough should be generously rewarded and celebrated.

Each dog is different. What is a positive consequence for one dog might be a negative consequence for another dog. For example, some dogs very much enjoy petting as a reward. For them, touch is a positive consequence. For other dogs, touch can be unpleasant or just neutral. Observe your dog closely to see how he feels about any consequence.

Be sure he's feeling as joyful as you want him to feel. If he's not, what do you need to adjust?

Negative Consequences

When a behavior results in *negative consequences*, the dog is *discouraged* from doing that behavior again. Negative consequences are used *sparingly*. Negative consequences are not pleasurable for the dog, but they do not need to involve pain, fear, or force.

A lot of old fashioned dog training used harsh, painful, or frightening negative consequences. Essentially, the message sent to the dog was, "Do this or else…" Relationship Centered Training does not use negative consequences in this way. The dog first must know how to be right, and that is achieved with positive consequences. A negative consequence can help clarify for the dog what is not right and, in that sense, can serve as meaningful information.

When I use negative consequences, I do so in the mildest possible way that is effective. To be unpleasant, a consequence does not have to be painful, harsh, scary, or threatening. It simply has to be something the dog does not wish to have happen again. That can be as mild as removing something that the dog wanted or hoped would happen.

For example, he may want you to throw his ball. You tell him DOWN but he ignores you. You tell him, "Too bad" (a verbal marker) and put the ball in your pocket for a while. That is a negative consequence. The dog does not want you to put the ball away.

What he learns is that nothing good comes from ignoring you. On the other hand, cooperating with you—lying down promptly when you ask—has the positive consequence of you throwing his ball.

You do have to give the dog another chance to be right so that he can see the contrast between the consequences of his choices. In the ball example, after a few seconds, I might once again ask the dog to lie down. If he does, I'd mark that verbally, praise him generously, pull the ball out of my pocket, and throw it for him. So the contrast becomes clear. Ignore the request to down and the ball is quietly put away; cooperate and the ball is thrown.

Here are some examples of negative consequences that give the dog useful information without scaring, threatening, or hurting him:

- loss of handler's attention (you may look away, turn your back, leave, interact with others)
- time-out (put on a tether, or in a crate, yard, other room)
- loss of freedom (not allowed to enter a space you are in)
- withdrawal of potential reward
- end of game/interaction

CHAPTER THIRTEEN

Using Rewards Effectively

Timing, intensity & variety make rewards rewarding

The growing tide of dog training that emphasizes positive reinforcement and humane techniques is something to celebrate. It is good to see dogs with their eyes bright, eager, trusting, and joyful.

There is a downside, however, to the positive training movement: confused handlers who intend to be positive, kind, and humane, but who are not skillful in using rewards effectively. They get stuck, and frustrated, wondering why being a "positive trainer" isn't enough and not understanding why.

Learning to use rewards effectively isn't difficult, but it gets challenging at best when trainers insist on drowning handlers in unnecessary technical jargon. It's not rocket surgery, and handlers already understand the concepts from their own life experience. They just don't know they know.

Effective rewards are closely tied in time to the desired behavior. The longer the delay between the behavior and the reward, the less likely the dog is to understand that behavior X is what resulted in the reward.

This is no different than someone thanking you for passing the salt. As long as the thanks is given close on the heels of the salt being passed, you're clear what the thanks is for. But if the thanks came 10 seconds later, you might be puzzled and have to think back to try to figure out what you were being thanked for. If you had done additional things for that person in those 10 seconds, such as pouring some water and passing the bread basket, you would be unclear if the thanks referred to all that you had done or just the last thing. Chances are very good you would not associate the thanks with passing the salt.

For most handlers and dogs, a good guideline is that a reward must occur within 2–3 seconds after the behavior. That sounds like a tight time frame, but, in behavioral terms, a lot can happen in 2–3 seconds. Try it. See how many gestures or things you can do while counting 1-2-3 slowly. Gives you a whole new appreciation for the value of timing! The more behaviors that your dog is offering, the more critical timing becomes in order to keep things clear.

Ideally, the reward should be given quickly and for a specific behavior only. A delay or lack of clarity can cause the dog to inadvertently perceive the reward as one given for another subsequent behavior or even a concurrent behavior. While teaching one of my dogs to bark at the back door to go out, I misjudged his response. I was so focused on getting a bark that I was ignoring his accompanying behavior of leaping around like a lunatic. When he finally did bark, I rewarded him instantly with praise and an open door. To my mind, mission accomplished. Unfortunately, he had been in mid-air when he barked and was rewarded. For quite a while afterwards, I had a dog who believed that the combination of leaping and barking was the behavior I wanted.

Timing is everything when trying to communicate precise concepts. Think of it as driving down a highway, waiting for a friend to tell you which exit you need to take. If her timing is excellent, you will choose the correct exit. If her timing is poor, you might hear, "Oh, *that* was our exit!" If she is unclear, you may miss the exit or misinterpret her communication to mean that the next exit is the one she desires. Inaccurate timing always confuses dogs. Learn to be clear, prompt, and accurate in your timing of rewards.

Intensity

The intensity of a reward is key to its effectiveness. In order to be effective, a consequence has to be *meaningful to the dog in that moment.* What may be a meaningful consequence in your quiet kitchen may not be useful at training class where your dog's attention is pulled in many directions by sights and sounds. At home, one small boring biscuit might do the trick and make your dog's eyes light up. In class, you may need to be much more interesting and use higher value treats.

I ask handlers, "Are you serving rice cakes or birthday cake?" Sheepishly, many realize they are using food rewards that are boring and bland, and serving them up with all the enthusiasm of a bored waitress. Nobody serves birthday cake that way! At any party worth attending, the cake is served in a way that says this is something special and good.

A reward's intensity is strictly dependent on the dog's perception of its intensity. A dog who does not particularly enjoy playing fetch would find a tennis ball a very low intensity reward (and possibly rate it as no reward at all). For a retrieving fanatic, you might not find anything that had greater intensity. I know dogs who would disregard entire steaks if their favorite bumper or ball were offered, and others who will accept a toy but far prefer food. Still others will pass up food or toys in exchange for exuberant, highly physical praise from their handler, eating the liver or grabbing the ball only after the emotional peak has passed. Each dog is an individual, and intensity of reward must be calibrated to each individual.

Intensity is also dependent on the frequency with which the reward is offered. A reward that the dog rates a very high intensity rarely loses its appeal, no matter how often it is used; lower intensity rewards can lose their appeal more quickly.

Novelty can increase the intensity of a reward. In my training classes, students are always amused that swapping treats with other students often results in their dogs being more interested in the new treats than the ones brought from home. The same is sometimes true for toys. However, for some dogs, novelty and unfamiliarity can be off putting, especially for nervous, anxious, or low confidence dogs.

To be effective, the intensity of the reward must also match the situation's degree of difficulty. A good guideline to follow is **the intensity/value of reward must be equal to or greater than the intensity of situation.**

Difficulty can be physical, mental, or emotional, as well as a combination of the three. A fearful dog who allows a stranger to exam her (high degree of emotional difficulty) should receive a reward of greater intensity than would a dog who found the entire exercise not particularly stressful or difficult. Learning a new task is far more difficult than performing a learned, habituated response. A breakthrough in training needs to be highlighted with intense, prolonged rewards.

Over a period of time, the appropriate pairing of reward intensity with the degree of difficulty results in a sliding scale approach to rewards. As a task becomes less difficult for the dog, less reward intensity is required to maintain that level of performance. It is not appropriate or useful to offer a fully-trained dog the same reward/intensity for sitting as you did when he was untrained and learning it all for the first time. This would be as silly as making a big deal over an adult signing his name for the thousandth time that year; though, such a fuss would be appropriate for a first-grader trying to master the basics of penmanship.

An intrinsically rewarding task is one that is naturally enjoyable to the dog or in line with his instinctual behavior. The dog finds the activity itself rewarding. For example, a retriever will retrieve almost endlessly; it's a behavior he enjoys without the need for much, if any, reward other than the activity itself.

But, less intrinsically rewarding tasks will require great reward intensity. If you are trying to teach a Scottish Deerhound to retrieve, the reward intensity may need to be high. This helps to offset the reality that Deerhounds, as a rule, do not particularly enjoy or see a purpose in running after objects and returning them to the careless owner who threw them away in the first place!

To improve and then maintain this retrieving behavior in a Deerhound, reward intensity will have to remain relatively high even when the behavior is learned. Since it deviates so drastically from his inherent behaviors, retrieving is a behavior that will probably rapidly deteriorate.

Simply put, the more a dog enjoys an activity in and of itself, the less reward intensity will be required to teach, improve, and maintain that behavior. Behavior at odds with the dog's prefer-

84 · SUZANNE CLOTHIER

ences may require higher intensity rewards in the teaching and maintenance of the behavior.

Variety

In addition to timing, variety matters a lot. Let's say your employer uses just one way to reward employees: a raise on a predictable timetable. How motivating is that to you? If you are like many people, you know that unless you really screw it up, the raise will occur. Regardless of the year-end speech of how much your hard work has been appreciated, chances are the reward occurs far too long after the action to be really motivational.

But what if your employer wandered by one afternoon, looked over your shoulder, and, thrilled with your work on a project, immediately handed you your coat and $100 with the best wishes for a pleasant afternoon off? What if, on a random basis, you received a 10% bonus in your weekly paycheck as a reward for a job well done in the last seven days? Or a T-shirt proclaiming you employee of the day? Or a new mug or small box of chocolates on your desk one morning with a note of thanks from the boss for working overtime?

Chances are good that you might find yourself more motivated to work harder. Why? Because they were true rewards—unseen before they arrived, unexpected, and novel in their variety.

Variety is the spice of life and the joy of using rewards. My dogs will work for food, for praise/petting, for tennis balls, sticks or Frisbees, and seem to live for the thrill of attacking a running garden hose. They will work especially hard for certain privileges that allow them to be with me, such as an only dog ride in the truck or the privilege of being barn dog for evening chores. Most important of all, they often do not know what the reward will be. I may call a younger dog from a play group and surprise her with some liver from my back pocket. Another time, I may call her and reward her with generous verbal praise and a long hug before sending her off to play again. Another day it may be a toy I found, or the chance to play tag together or simply share an exuberant "good dog" dance. It's never just the same old liver or ball or anything. It's a variety of rewards.

Frequently, handlers tell me that their dog only works for balls, or food, or whatever. They are serious! Stretching the example a little, imagine a husband who tells you that only diamonds make his wife happy. Wouldn't you question that relationship? Either the wife is very shallow and limited in her definitions of pleasurable experiences, or the husband offers no "rewards" but diamonds.

In my experience, handlers whose dogs work for only one reward do so because they have taught the dog that a ball or a treat or whatever is the only reward. It is up to the handler to discover as many ways to please, excite, thrill, and motivate the dog as possible and use them all as rewards when training. A dog must understand that this is a reward. My dogs all grow up learning that silly games are fun, and fun is always a useful reward. (Be cautious before deciding that you too will now reward your previously food/toy-trained dog with silly games. You may end up leaping around like a fool while the dog stares at you in amazement, wondering what the heck happened to his liver treat or Frisbee!)

The more rewards you have at your disposal, the more training you can do in almost any situation. You don't need to hunt up that special treat or toy or whatever; you can use as a reward nothing more than your own excitement, sincere pleasure, and a willingness to entertain your dog with a silly game of tag.

Handlers have a tendency to lean on just one or two rewards without realizing that may, in certain circumstances, seriously limit their ability to communicate to the dog how well he did. If, for example, you rely on tennis balls and verbal praise, what happens when your dog is 13, deaf, and unable to chase a ball? What happens if *you* lose your voice or cannot throw a ball? If I were able to move nothing more than my facial muscles, I'd still have some useful rewards left, since my dogs have learned many silly games revolving around blinks and winks and changes of expression.

At one of my training camps, we did a "silent" training—a standard obedience routine where handlers are completely silent. Half of the dogs actually became scared and very confused. Another quarter of the dogs, while anxious, could get sufficient clues from smiles and body posture to keep working, though the relief on their faces was palpable when the handlers regained their voices. The remaining dogs had no problem working as usual, since their handlers had always relied on many different forms of communicating and rewarding.

Generosity

Get creative. Develop your own tool kit of rewards of varying intensities (everything from a simple "thanks" to a singing telegram of "Wow! What a dog!") and modalities: touch, taste, smell, hearing, sight, tenderness, excitement, laughter, active, passive, freedom, and all the many wondrous things that make your dog glad that he's alive. This may be as simple as a good hug for your Bassett and then a long walk where he's allowed to sniff the world to his heart's content with nary a "No sniff" to be heard. It may mean throwing that ball 20 times more than you really wanted to, because your dog loves that best of all. If you pay attention, you and your dog will discover that the world is full of rewards, the greatest of which is simply being together.

CHAPTER FOURTEEN

The Power of Social Interactions as Rewards

Put down the cookies for a moment;
See how powerful social interaction can be

A trainer friend asked me, "Do you use treats when working with a dog who is worried, fearful, reactive, or otherwise having trouble, or do you use social contact (voice tone, touch, etc.) as the reward? I am certain that *it depends* is an important part of the answer. But, what do you use most frequently?"

I had to chuckle. **It Depends** is my bumper sticker for life. Most of all, it depends on what the dog says works for him in the moment. But how specifically to achieve that?

First, we back up a bit to the first of my *Elemental Questions*™: "Hello?"

By beginning here, at the most elemental point of any relationship, I am asking the animal if he would be interested in a conversation. Answers range from *Yes!* to *maybe* to *No* or *go away, you're scaring me* to *go away or I will bite you.* And all shades in between.

What I do after that initial question has been asked depends very much on the answer I get from the dog. Let's focus on normal dogs without any intense fear, irritation, anger, or frustration, who are not asocial or simply disinterested in people. Let's assume the dog has said, "Okay. I could consider a conversation with you."

Initially, I frequently employ a strong combination of very high value treats **plus** *always*, forever, no exception, *the real deal* of authentic engagement: social interaction. This is built of eye contact, body language, voice, breathing, intensity, movement, and touch. The specific combination I create is tailored to that specific dog. The dog's behavior drives my behavior. The combination is adjusted (as fast as I am humanly capable) to keep it effective for that dog in that moment.

Regardless of the specific combo, however, one thing quickly becomes apparent to the dog: I am really present for him, really alert to him, and adjusting my behavior based on what he does. This is powerful stuff for any social animal. Think how *you* feel when someone really pays attention to you, really listens to you.

Long before I work with a dog on something specific, however, I use some of the other *Elemental Questions*™. "Who are you?" leads me to assess what he finds valuable and interesting. I observe how he utilizes space socially, what he does in response to me and my body language, eye contact, movements, and voice, and his response to the treats (or toys) available. The answers to this *Elemental Question*™ provide a starting point from which I move into working with him.

All of that can happen really fast. And it can keep changing, moment to moment.

How much the social interaction means, of course, depends on the individual dog and that relationship. It wouldn't matter much if a stranger told you how wonderful you were and gave you $100 bills as he told you. The money (a non-social reward) would have value, but a stranger's opinion of you? Not so much. Coming from someone who matters a great deal to you, the money would still have value, but their good opinion of you may be far more valuable—and have longer lasting impact—than any non-social reward.

Conversely, there are things that you would find so difficult or scary or unpleasant that even from a beloved friend, praise or encouragement alone would not be sufficient; the equation would need to be balanced out with some heavy-duty reinforcements. A trusted friend who was also handing you $100 bills could probably get you to work through even difficult stuff, unless you were very afraid or felt deeply unsafe.

The inherent power of social interaction is wildly underestimated by trainers, I think. Dogs tell me I'm quite right about this one. I often have the same treats as the handler, but what I offer that the dog finds so valuable is the social interaction provided at a high degree of coherence and congruity. Everything in me truly says to the dog that I'm working to connect with him, that he really matters to me in the now moment we are sharing.

Finding the appropriate balance of social interaction plus non-social rewards depends very much on several factors.

The handler must be both willing and able to invest himself in an authentic way. Coherence, congruity, and continuity matter to dogs, just as they do to people. You must be lined up body/mind/soul with what you're intending to offer the dog through your connection. Incongruous, disconnected, or incoherent intent and actions will make any intelligent creature doubtful of the value of interacting with you.

The relationship and social interaction must have value for the dog. People would like to think it is automatically so, but it isn't always. In some situations, the social aspect counts for a lot, in other situations, not much.

In the case of fear and anxiety, understand that trust, respect, and the relationship only go so far. If these went as far as some trainers seem to think they do, none of us would be afraid of snakes or spiders once a trusted and beloved friend showed us how wonderful snakes and spiders are. Respecting the fear or anxiety as separate from the relationship is critical. The relationship can be an important *support*, but it cannot be superimposed over the fear/anxiety in order to erase the fear.

I am always deeply saddened by people who say, "If only he trusted me more, he would know he was safe," in a situation where the dog clearly felt anything but safe. No question the handler means well, and wishes to help the dog, but, in misunderstanding what the relationship can and cannot do, they may fail the dog in a big way without meaning to.

Social interaction can be a serious, unwelcome, and unhappy pressure for many dogs, so it must be used with care and with respect to what the dog has to say about it. Here's a parallel. You're really worried about something, and a well-meaning friend keeps telling you, "It's okay, I'm here for you, you can do this, it's all fine, have a cookie, you're doing great, we're going to get thru this blah, blah, blah. . ." non-stop till you want to scream. That kind of interaction just adds to your stress and does not help in any way, however well-intentioned the friend might be.

Just like people, dogs differ in what they find supportive. Some find a gentle, quiet flow of information comforting and helpful. Others really need the mental, emotional, and/or physical space to be able to think and process. Ask the dog what works for him, and then do that, no matter what your individual preferences or style might be. While you might find comfort in soothing words, your dog might not; while you might prefer to be alone, he may not. Ask the dog!

Whatever the species, social beings recognize the authenticity of someone trying to connect, trying hard to listen to them. It's understood, appreciated, and best of all, always available—a genuine connection from who we are to who that animal is in the moment.

CHAPTER FIFTEEN

Aggression: Possible Causes

Some of the many factors behind the behaviors labeled as aggression

Aggression is a very big label that covers a lot of territory. Barking, growling, snarling, lunging, snapping, biting are all behaviors we may label as aggression. Simply labeling a dog's behavior as aggressive is not informative or helpful.

Many of the dogs presented to me are already labeled as "aggressive." Looked at carefully, it turns out that many of these dogs are quite fair about offering warning signs, and many of these dogs are desperately seeking to avoid a confrontation. Unfortunately, their actions are either missed until quite dramatic, or the behaviors are wildly misinterpreted, leading to poor responses by the mistaken humans involved.

How frustrating that must be for the dog when people have not been able to accurately read the signals the dog is sending. For some dogs, there are no other options but to escalate their own behavior in order to make their message clear.

Sadly, the dogs sometimes pay with their lives for human misunderstanding of these communications. While there are dogs who do wish to do harm, most dogs I have met are trying desperately to communicate in a way where they can be heard.

Observation or Interpretation?

To understand aggression or any other label assigned to canine behavior, we need to back up a bit to the difference between observation and interpretation.

"Aggressive" is an interpretation made after behaviors are observed, just as you might assess someone as "friendly" because they smiled at you, held the door open for you, and wished you a good day. Telling me that you thought someone was friendly (an interpretation) does not detail what that person did or did not do. Interpretation and labels do not help you understand what may be going on in the dog's mind. Interpretations cannot be observed, and their meaning can vary significantly from person to person.

Observation (not interpretation) of behavior means that if there were video of the event available, you would be able to show someone else the precise behavior that you saw. "There! That's when the dog stopped moving, turned his head, growled, and then lunged to bite her hand twice before he moved away to the other side of the table." No matter who was watching it, the observed behaviors would be the same.

Be specific about the behaviors you observe, and build a careful picture based on your observations. Describe in detail the situation in which the behavior was presented, and the dog's body language and posture. "When this was happening, the handler did X, and then the dog did Y."

How, when, where, with whom, and in what context the dog offers the behavior are critical clues.

Avoid assumptions, labels, or the use of non-specific language like "he freaked out." Be specific. For example, does "freaked out" mean the dog bolted away, crashed into the wall, and only then lunged forward with loud barks? Or that the dog's pupils dilated dramatically, with ears laid back tight, and then he lunged forward with a snap? Or that he just barked 10 times?

Details and Differences

The difference between aggression springing from one reason rather than another lies in the details of the dog's behavior and body language. If you like, consider that each type of aggression has typical symptoms that any interested handler can learn to recognize. Knowing what to do to resolve the problem is another story. Seek a professional trainer's help when dealing with aggression.

The following sections outline some of the details of the many behaviors that may all be labeled as aggressive but represent very different behaviors and body language motivation, and, of course, require different solutions. Possible solutions are briefly outlined; this is not a detailed treatise on resolving aggression in its many forms.

Pain-induced Response

Typical symptoms:

- The dog actively resists and/or growls when the handler tries to force, correct, or even gently model him into position. This pain-based response may be seen if the handler asks for quicker sit by correcting or pushing down on the dog's back or pelvis, or tries to roll the dog over on one hip for long down, etc.
- The dog objects to having a collar or head-halter put on, a leash connected to the collar or head-halter, and equipment removed.
- If corrected by leash and/or collar, the dog comes up the lead immediately upon receiving the correction.

- If physically handled or maneuvered, the dog swings his head towards the handler or tries to move away from the handler.
- The dog may yelp or scream, and do nothing more. But the dog may also growl, snarl, snap at, or actually bite the handler.

In all cases, there is a clear connection between physical handling and/or correction and the dog's response. In the case of a very sensitive dog, the response may occur in anticipation of being touched, handled, restrained, or corrected.

Possible causes, treatment, solutions:

- Know the physical problems that are common to your breed(s) and be alert to them. For example, hip or elbow dysplasia, OCD, patella problems, cruciate ruptures, spinal problems, breathing disorders, etc. may be playing a role in the dog's behavior. Professionals should be familiar with the issues typical for the breeds in their practice. Always refer physical problems to the dog's veterinarian.
- If the dog is sore in any given area, a pain response may be seen. Even if the joints or the muscles are normally conformed, there can still be soft tissue pain. Just like us, dogs can have too much fun, overdo on special occasions, slip or fall, or have a modest accident that leaves them feeling uncomfortable. Involve the veterinarian.
- For large breed dogs who are still growing, consider panosteitis (a disease of the growing dog). These dogs will especially resent having long bones of the legs grabbed or handled. Other development disorders can also create pain responses. Have the veterinarian examine the dog.
- Know what normal, healthy movement looks like. Take time to watch the dog moving. Does he look comfortable,

smooth and easy in his movement? If the dog is exhibiting signs of physical discomfort, have the veterinarian examine the dog. (See our video, *Your Athletic Dog: A Functional Approach,* for a detailed approach to understanding gait and movement.)

- Tick-borne diseases can leave dogs with pain in the joints and throughout the body. Ask the veterinarian to test for tick-borne diseases to rule out this possible cause.

- Tonsillitis, ear infections, even tooth pain can make a dog sensitive to any touch or tightening of equipment around the head, neck, and ears. A veterinary check is needed.

- Touch sensitivity can create disproportionate responses to what a handler believes is a fair, gentle, appropriate touch. Some dogs may actually show anticipatory behavior and shriek, cry out, or warn *prior* to the actual touch. For these dogs, handlers will have to adjust any touch to be within the dog's limits; desensitization and/or counter-conditioning may be helpful unless there is a sensory processing disorder.

- Correction based training has many drawbacks, not the least of which is that physical corrections can be painful for the dog. Have the handler moderate physical signals if correction based training is used; an ideal correction is the mildest signal that will be instructive for the dog. However, I far prefer to encourage handlers to learn training methods that do not require physical corrections.

- The collar may be providing too much physical stimulation. Dogs differ in their sensitivity to equipment. Avoid using painful collars (choke, prong, shock, or electric). Use milder collars such as martingale type or flat buckle collars, or avoid collars altogether and switch to a well-fitted body harness.

- Damage to or soreness in the neck can create strong reactions. Switch to a well-fitted body harness. Avoid head halters and front-pull harness as these can create soft-tissue problems due to the abnormal postures and pulling they can encourage.

Regardless of the source of the pain, do not assume that simply stopping the painful input will restore the dog to balance. The dog may benefit from the healing power of veterinary-guided physical therapy, chiropractic, acupuncture, massage, TTouch, and other forms of bodywork. All can be useful, natural adjuncts to helping a painful dog.

Re-directed Aggression

Typical symptoms:

Re-directed aggression is seen in situations where the dog is highly aroused by another dog, animal, or person, and frustrated because he can't get to the object of his focus. Re-direction can be an extremely dangerous situation, as some dogs are quite violent when re-directing and may bite hard and repeatedly.

Barking at windows, fences, from within vehicles, or behind other barriers can result in re-direction, with the target being any person, dog, or animal in the immediate vicinity. Sometimes, the dog will redirect onto nearby inanimate objects, such as vegetation, curtains, or furniture.

Some dogs will also redirect when on-leash, turning on their handler and/or other dogs being walked with them.

Any interference by the handler, including simple attempts to attract the dog's attention by offering food, toys, or just reaching into the dog's visual field can cause re-direction. Physical contact with the dog, such as leash corrections or hands-on corrections such as collar grabs, scruff shakes, muzzle grabs, or slaps may result in the dog re-directing his frustration onto handler.

Possible causes, treatment, solutions:
- Ideally, prevent or avoid any situations that could possibly trigger a re-direction episode.
- Pulling on leash is contributory. The dog who is allowed to pull on leash is both disconnected from the handler, out of control, and already in an aroused state. Add the trigger of another dog, animal, or person, and the problem escalates fast. Insist on loose leash walking from all dogs.
- Damage control is necessary. Remove yourself and others from the dog's vicinity, if possible. Once the dog is able to think clearly, gain his voluntary cooperation in any way possible; do not use force to remove the dog.

Rudeness by Other Dogs

Typical symptoms:

The dog noisily warns, makes dramatic snapping or "clacking" with snarls towards another dog, or actually nips or bites another dog who has gotten into his space.

The telltale clue is always that this is a dog responding to rudeness, not seeking a confrontation. The dog acting "aggressively" is often responding to an invasion of his space by the other dog. Invasion of space by another dog, even one that is friendly, is a common trigger for many dogs.

Many sporting breeds have been selectively bred to be very tolerant of other dogs—a wonderful quality in a companion dog. Ironically, that quality of dog-to-dog tolerance is likely to lead the friendly dog to inadvertently trigger responses in dogs who have a bigger personal space, such as terriers, and working and guarding breeds (or individual dogs of any breed).

Whatever the breed(s) involved, handlers are at fault when their dog triggers an aggressive response. Handlers often allow their dog to invade the space of other dogs in the mistaken notion their dog is friendly and means no harm. While they may be right about their dogs meaning no harm, they do not understand that other breeds are not as welcoming of even well-intentioned space invaders. Sadly, they also do not recognize that the "aggressive" dog is responding, not initiating the conflict.

Possible causes, treatment, solutions:

Be sure all handlers in your group or class know the basics of rude/polite dog behavior, which includes:

- Interrupt and, if necessary, block any sustained eye contact that lasts more than a few seconds, even across the room.
- Do not allow your dog to approach another dog without explicit permission from the other dog's handler.
- Do not allow your dog to approach another dog who is in a crate; behind a fence, door, or other barrier; or in a pen.
- Know where your dog is at all times, and know what's in his line of sight.

Keep the dog(s) who caused the incident on a long line and under close supervision when working on recalls or long distance stays.

Keep the dog who responded to the rudeness well-protected by barriers or people between him and the rude dog.

All handlers have an obligation to protect other dogs from their own dog's "friendliness!" While anyone can be surprised once or twice, it does become your responsibility to learn how to avoid problems in the future.

If necessary, assign red bandanas to dogs needing extra space. This serves as a warning to other handlers that the Red Bandana dog should be given room and to not let their dogs, however friendly, interact without specific invitation by the Red Bandana dog's handler.

Resource Guarding and Rule Setting

Resource guarding is another broadly applied—and often inaccurate—label that gets dogs in a world of trouble, even put to sleep. Simply put, resource guarding is about the dog's anxiety that something he values will be taken away, and his attempts to warn others away from his possession.

By dog law, possession really is nine-tenths of the law. A dog is entitled to try to retain anything he has in his possession, regardless of who is asking him to give it up. The smallest four-week old puppy can growl, keep his bone, and turn away from an adult male, and be acting perfectly appropriately by canine standards.

Human expectations that we have the right to take whatever we want whenever we want put us at odds with the dog's natural behavior. Understandably, dogs can get aggressive when we act in ways that would be wildly inappropriate among canines. The dog's anxiety can exacerbate the situation further.

Rule setting differs from resource guarding in significant ways. The same dog law "what's mine is mine" applies, but with these significant differences:

- the dog is acting out of confidence, not anxiety or fear
- the item need not be closely held or guarded but can be at a considerable distance from the "owner"
- the dog maintains his possession of the item initially through psychological means, such as giving others "the eye," and resorting to threats and physicality only if necessary

Typical symptoms:

The resource guarding dog is typically positioned very near the place, thing, or person/animal being guarded, with the overall body language compressed and often quite still. The perceived threat will receive sideways glances (usually eyes do the moving, not the head, resulting in "whale eye"). The head may be lowered (slightly or dramatically) with the muzzle, chin, and even throat and part of the chest over the object.

The rule-setting dog is typically positioned in a comfortable place not necessarily near the object of possession, but one that offers a clear line of sight to the possession. The dog may appear quite relaxed and unconcerned until someone is very close to his possession, at which point he will become very alert and react.

Possible causes, treatment, solutions:

- The resource guarding dog requires an approach that, first and foremost, relieves his anxiety about losing his possession, and, secondly, teaches him to willingly relinquish a possession when asked. Avoid any approach that involves punishing the dog, fails to address his anxiety, or relies on tricking the dog into leaving his possession that is then quickly snatched away before he can return. Good approaches relieve the dog's anxiety while also teaching surrender of objects.

- The rule-setting dog must be addressed within the context of the relationships within the household. Typically, there is an imbalance between the human(s) and the dog. A clearer structure is needed for the relationships, including how this dog may set rules for others.

Resistance

Sometimes, aggression follows closely on the heels of resistance, especially when handlers ignore the importance of resistance as meaningful information.

Resistance or refusal to cooperate are important communications that can spring from many causes: confusion, anxiety, boredom, lack of motivation, physical inability, lack of respect for the handler, being overwhelmed, the training methodology, and specific equipment.

Typical symptoms:

The dog may actively resist being handled or even gently modeled into position by the handler (e.g., tucked into sit or down) by growling, snapping, biting, wrestling, pushing the handler away with his feet, and mouthing the handler's arms and hands. The dog may be saying that the handler has not earned the right to handle him in such ways. This does not mean that if a dog respects the handler that any kind of handling will—or should—be tolerated; handlers still owe dogs respectful, appropriate handling.

Possible causes, treatment, solutions:

- Pain-related responses must be ruled out.
- Kinesthetic (touch) input provides too much stimulation; find ways to gain cooperation without physical guidance.
- If the dog is confused, work in smaller slices so the dog can understand and be successful rapidly and frequently.
- For the bored dog, stop boring him! Focus on skill mastery rather than repetitions; consider switching to activities that the dog actually enjoys.
- Lack of motivation is a frequent cause of resistance. Be sure that consequences are used wisely and well. Believe the dog when he tells you it's not worth it, and make it worth his while!
- The overwhelmed or anxious dog needs support, less pressure, time to process information, and smaller slices so he can succeed rapidly and frequently. Work to alleviate the anxiety and build confidence.
- Any equipment or technique that uses an application of force may elicit reflexive resistance from a dog. This includes equipment often considered to be humane, such as head halters which—however gently!—physically force the dog to comply. Poorly fitted equipment can create discomfort and resistance, but even well-fitted equipment can be uncomfortable for the dog. If the method or equipment creates resistance, stop using it; find another way.
- Lack of respect for the handler needs to be addressed in a broad, systematic way that encompasses the entire relationship, such as Puppy Politeness Poker and focus on Control-Connection-Permission, in addition to the specific training skills that may be needed.
- Physical inability can take many forms, ranging from the dog feeling unsure about his ability to accurately control his body to outright limitations—"I can't do that"—due to

physical issues. Learn how to perform a functional assessment and involve a sports medicine-knowledgeable veterinarian.

In the immediate moment, when faced with resistance, do not force the issue; find a reasonable compromise. Forcing the resistant dog does not always lead to aggression, but when it does, the dog's trust in the relationship is affected. Find a way to address the resistance and avoid the dog feeling the need to underline how he's feeling by escalating to more dramatic behaviors.

Over-stimulation

Typical symptoms:

Many dogs respond to overstimulation by using their mouth to grab at the handler's arms, hands, legs, feet, clothing, lead, etc. This is often not aggression but a response to too much stimuli; attempts to use force or corrections only pour fuel on the fire.

The stimulation may come from many sources: the environment, sensory input, training equipment, the handler and/or other people, corrections, toys, treats, other dogs or animals, the pressures of a specific situation, frustration, excitement, or any combination of these.

The over-stimulated dog often leaps up, grabbing and releasing, sometimes bouncing off the person, and, if free to do so, may run around the person and do "drive-by" grabs of clothing, hands, and legs. He may not offer any significant vocalizations other than whining, short frustration barks, or brief growls. Sustained growls are typically absent. There is a frantic, wild quality to the dog's movements.

While there is usually no real threat here, the dog can become increasingly frustrated and begin to grab harder or bear down with greater pressure. How much damage the dog does will depend heavily on the dog's bite inhibition.

Possible causes, treatment, solutions:

- The dog may have sensitivity to some sensory input, such as sights or sounds. Conversely, there may be some sensory deficits that lead the dog to over-react.

- Recognizing the triggering stimuli is key. It may be necessary to eliminate the trigger, or adjust the intensity, duration, or distance. (See Chapter Ten, *Understanding Thresholds,* for detailed information.)

- Punishing the dog with sprays, using aversives, such as an air horn, or trying to use physical corrections often escalates the frustration and results in the dog offering *more*, not less, of the unwanted behavior.

- Move the dog to a "cool down zone" that offers a visual barrier and/or much more distance from other dogs/animals.

- Work quietly, being careful not to use physical praise, big and/or fast hand movements, or an excited voice. Your goal should be to lower the dog's arousal; the mouthing is secondary to that primary issue of non-productive arousal.

- If using rewards that can be triggers that over-stimulate the dog, take care to use them in useful ways and teach the dog that there are rules for his behavior even in the presence of these exciting stimuli. Handlers often eliminate rewards that the dog finds intensely stimulating ("Oh, he just gets too excited for me to use X") instead of using this powerful reinforcer with skill and to good effect.

Fear-based Social Responses

Typical symptoms:

A fear-based response is usually seen when the dog is being approached by other dogs or people, or when someone enters the dog's environment. An initial response may be to try to avoid the approaching person/dog, but, if unable to leave, held on leash, or perhaps pulled forward by the handler and forced to remain in the situation, the dog may shift to defensive aggression. Typically, the dog will move forward with dramatic gestures—barking, snarling, and other behaviors intended to make the interaction stop and to drive the intruder away—while body posture and details, such as ears, tail, facial expression, and overall compression indicate a fear-based response.

Possible causes, treatment, solutions:

- A lack of appropriate socialization is often at the root of this behavior. While commonly heard advice is to "just keep socializing him!" the reality is that repeated exposures do not automatically confer confidence, success, or a reduction in fear. My approach, Mindful Socialization, focuses on keeping the dog well within his Think & Learn Zone, and on the quality of all experiences with the goal of the dog feeling safe and successful.

- Protecting the dog from being overwhelmed or pressured by other dogs is the handler's responsibility. Use a red bandana on the fearful dog to remind others that the dog needs space. Be a strong advocate for your dog. Do not hesitate to step in and help your dog in social settings, even if that means you might offend handlers who allow their dogs to upset your dog. Work carefully on trying to build the fearful dog's skills for dealing with other dogs. Counter-conditioning, desensitization and careful socialization can help.

- For the dog who is afraid of people, do not put the dog in triggering situations, or any situation that is beyond the dog's coping skills. When in doubt, **always remove the dog from the situation to avoid a biting incident.** The dog will pay the price (sometimes with his life) for being pushed past his ability to cope. Build the dog's skills in dealing with people using my Treat/Retreat program, counter-conditioning, and desensitization.

CHAPTER SIXTEEN

He Just Wants To Say "Hi!"

Aggression or appropriate response to rudeness?

Sitting quietly on the mall bench beside my husband, I was minding my own business when the man approached. I glanced up as the man sat next to me. He was a bit close for my comfort, so I edged a little closer to my husband who, busy reading a book, ignored me. Still feeling a bit uncomfortable with the strange man so close, I then turned my head slightly away from him, politely indicating I was not interested in any interaction. To my horror, the man leaned over me and began licking my neck while rudely groping me.

When I screamed and pushed him away, my trouble really began. My husband angrily threw me to the ground, yelling at me "Why did you do that? He was only trying to be friendly and say *hi!* What a touchy witch you are! You're going to have to learn to behave better in public."

People all around us stared and shook their heads sadly. I heard a few murmuring that they thought my husband should do something about my behavior; some even mentioned that he shouldn't have such a violent woman out in public until I'd been trained better. As my husband dragged me to the car, I noticed that the man who had groped me had gone a bit further down the mall and was doing the same thing to other women.

This is a silly scenario, isn't it? First, anyone who knows me knows that I would never be in a mall except under considerable duress. More seriously, no rational human being would consider my response to the man's rudeness as inappropriate or vicious. By invading my personal space, the man crossed the lines of decent, civilized behavior; my response would be considered quite justified.

That my husband might punish me for responding to such rudeness by screaming and pushing the offender away is perhaps the most ridiculous aspect of this scenario. If he were to act in this way, there would be no doubt in the minds of even the most casual observers that his ego was of far greater importance than my safety or comfort, and that he was sorely lacking even rudimentary empathy for how I might be feeling in this situation.

Fortunately for me, this scenario is completely imaginary. Unfortunately for many dogs, it is a very real scenario that is repeated far too often. Inevitably, as the owners who have allowed their dogs to act rudely retreat from the situation, there are comments made about "that aggressive dog" (the dog whose space had been invaded) and the classic comment, usually said in hurt tones, "He only wanted to say hi."

Close Call

Years ago, a friend of mine in Texas placed a Greyhound with a supposedly knowledgeable person in the Northeast. This person gives seminars all over the world on the care and training of a certain animal, so my friend felt comfortable placing this wonderful hound with her. Less than one week later, my friend received a hysterical call in which the supposed expert was threatening to have this Greyhound put to sleep for being aggressive. Since I was the closest resource, my Texan friend asked me to see what I could do, making it clear that this was one of the best Greyhounds that she had ever rescued—he had demonstrated incredible tolerance for all other dogs and animals.

When I spoke with the new owner, I asked what was going on. Her response was sadly classic. "Well, Champ is quite aggressive. For example, he'll just be lying on the dog bed and my two Goldens come over to say *hi* and then he just attacks them. It's awful!"

My first tip-off that the Greyhound was totally blameless was her comment that the Goldens were just coming over to say "hi." Generally speaking, dogs who live together don't walk over to each other to repeatedly say hello, no more than every time you walk in a room you walk over to family members and say hello by getting right into their face.

Further questioning revealed that the body posture of the two Goldens while saying "hi" was very upright, ears forward, tails up and wagging very slowly—a confrontational stance, not a greeting. The Greyhound often initially turned his head away, but, when the two Goldens began sniffing at him and poking him, he would growl softly. Then, as they persisted, the hound would finally leap up with a roar. Despite her hysterical descriptions of the "fights," I was able to get her to define the amount of damage done by the Greyhound—none.

As we talked on, the picture became clearer. The two Goldens were quite spoiled, pushy with other dogs, and decidedly not happy with a new dog in their household. The woman cheerfully admitted that the two Goldens were not too well-trained and she sometimes had trouble controlling them around other animals, but, she added, "They are so sweet, and there isn't an aggressive bone in their bodies!"

The Greyhound, on the other hand, she viewed as a fierce and aggressive, a dangerous animal who she now had muzzled at all times. I thought for a bit about trying to educate this woman about dog behavior but decided the kindest thing to do for this hound was to just go and rescue him. So I did. By the time I'd driven home with this incredible dog, he'd been renamed Beckett and stayed with me for almost two years until I placed him with a friend who adores him. As for his "aggression," I never saw a hint of it in any situation.

While there are many frustrating aspects of being a dog trainer, one of the most disturbing scenarios is the situation where a dog is acting appropriately but is nonetheless punished (in the name of "training") by humans who do not understand what constitutes normal canine behavior and responses.

Sadly, normal behavior is quickly labeled "problem" behavior, and the dog becomes a "problem dog." Depending on the skill and awareness of the trainer or instructor, the dog may be merely puzzled or irritated by well-meaning attempts to desensitize or re-condition the behavior or actually punished quite severely using any number of horrific and senseless techniques.

In Beckett's case, a lack of understanding nearly cost him his life. Had I not intervened, his extremely uninformed owner would have had him put to sleep as aggressive. In most cases, the true problem—the rude dog and rude owner who allowed his dog to be rude—is not recognized or addressed.

Strange Behavior or Normal Dog?

This following is an actual email from a concerned owner (re-printed by permission). While I've changed details in order to protect the innocent (the dog!), it is an excellent example of an owner who has tried hard to do well with and for her dog, and of instructors who mean well but fail on a very deep level when it comes to understanding normal canine interactions.

(Note: This email haunted me for several days, long after I had answered the dog's owner. I knew this was such a common but misunderstood problem that I felt I needed to write this article. This article has been distributed worldwide!)

Dear Suzanne:

You don't know me, but L. is a friend of mine, and she suggested I write to you regarding the strange behavior of my dog. I have a female (spayed) golden retriever, 3 years old, named Cream. Cream comes from good lines (champion show) and is "almost" your typical golden: sweet, goofy, lovable, loves ALL people. Recently, Cream became a certified therapy dog through the Delta Society.

Yet Cream has one problem: she hates young, hyper dogs. If a dog starts jumping all over Cream, Cream gets aggressive—starts to growl, shows some teeth, and if the dog doesn't take the hint after a few seconds, Cream will "attack" the dog. Every time this has happened, it's happened very quickly, and I get Cream off the dog immediately (and "correct" her—laying her down, holding her muzzle, shaking her a bit, saying "NO!" very sternly, etc.). Cream doesn't even like young dogs to lick her—she snaps at them if they do.

Now, Cream only displays this aggressive behavior with young, hyper dogs. Cream has regular dog pals that she plays with almost daily—they wrestle, play bite, and run around together. Some of the dogs she plays with are older, some are the same age, some are even younger, the youngest now being about 9 months old. She plays with both sexes, but she does seem to prefer males. (Cream was spayed at 10 months.)

Cream is in good health. She's on a raw foods diet, had titer testing this year instead of vaccinations, had a full blood panel and thyroid check and both were fine, has been CERFed and her eyes are fine. She does have some mild hip dysplasia, but it doesn't bother her, and she shows no symptoms. She's been very well-socialized since she's been a dog, and I bring her everywhere I can (shopping malls, parks, sometimes to campus).

Cream has been through lots of obedience classes, beginning when she was a dog at 4 months old in puppy kindergarten. For the past several months she's been going through a basic obedience class with young dogs—I've been trying to recondition her behavior towards young dogs. I've been food rewarding her when she shows no aggressive behavior to a dog.

It's been going okay, but two weeks ago, a young mastiff puppy got away from her owner, and came charging at Cream. She crashed into Cream (and it was just because she was over excited—she wasn't being aggressive) and Cream came up growling and snarling. Then last weekend, a black lab dog did the same thing, and Cream had the same reaction. Throughout the class, Cream won't even look at the dog—has her back turned toward them the entire time.

I've got the dog trainers of the class stumped, as they don't really know what to do. Cream is normally such a sweet dog, good with commands, great with people. Cream is also wonderful with children, and has an endless supply of patience with kids—they can pull on her ears, hug her tightly, pull on her tail —and Cream loves it. Cream is fine with dogs who are calm, even friendly towards them, with her tail wagging, and she might even try to get them to play.

Cream has had some bad experiences with dogs. A pit bull jumped out of a car when we were on a walk, and attacked Cream (Cream was about 7 months old). She's had dogs run out of houses and attack her, and dogs who were supposedly tied up, get loose and attack her.

So, do you have any suggestions or theories for us? Well, I'd really appreciate any thoughts you have on our situation.

Lee Anne

Lee Anne tried to be as thorough as possible in presenting Cream's case to me. Her concern was evident; based on what she presented, she was an owner who spent a lot of time working with and training her dog. From my point of view, the picture she painted was a clear one. Cream was a perfectly normal dog who, from time to time, was forced by rude dogs to draw a line and inform them precisely how rude they had been.

Unfortunately for Cream, her appropriate response to rudeness was misread as aggression, and she was punished. I cannot even begin to fully comprehend the confusion that must flood a dog who has acted appropriately but is punished nonetheless.

"If a dog starts jumping all over Cream, Cream gets aggressive—starts to growl, shows some teeth, and if the dog doesn't take the hint after a few seconds, Cream will 'attack' the dog."

There is clear evidence here that Cream never did "suddenly attack" anyone. In a normal progression of warning signs, Cream gave the offending dog a chance to back off. It is only when warning signs were ignored that Cream had to escalate to the threat of violence. That is all her "attacks" on any dog were—threats, not actual attacks with the intent to do harm. Dogs who mean to do harm do so with breathtaking speed, and intervention is generally not possible. Though noisy and scary, most "fights" are a series of ritualized threats with fully-inhibited biting employed by the combatants.

When I had a phone consultation with Lee Anne, one of my first questions was about Cream's "attacks" on other dogs. I wanted to know how much damage she did to the other dog during these "attacks." In his lectures on aggression, Dr. Ian Dunbar urges trainers to always look at what he calls the Fight-Bite Ratio: how many altercations has your dog been involved in, and how many times has another dog been seriously hurt by your dog?

Dunbar is careful to define "seriously hurt" as needing veterinary attention. An accidental puncture or two on the muzzle, head, or ear is not a serious injury, merely a by-product of powerful teeth flashing at speed as the dog tries to make his point in a very noisy, dramatic way. The majority of dog-to-dog altercations do not result in serious injury, though they are extremely frightening to witness. Even if the number of fights is quite high, if the number of bites inflicted in those fights is low or zero, then you know that the dog is inhibiting his bite—a good sign even though there may be problems that cause the fights and need resolution.

For all of Cream's "attacks" on other dogs, there had only been one small puncture inflicted on the head, a typical site for an accidental, unintended punch of a tooth. As I suspected from her owner's description, Cream had been well-socialized with both people and other dogs and had learned to inhibit her bite. Thus, her "attacks," while alarming to all involved, did not result in any damage to the offending dog.

"*. . .two weeks ago, a young mastiff puppy got away from her owner, and came charging at Cream. She crashed into Cream (and it was just because she was over excited—she wasn't being aggressive) and Cream came up growling and snarling. Then last weekend, a black lab dog did the same thing, and Cream had the same reaction.*"

Hidden in this section of Lee Anne's letter is an important notion that dogs aren't acting rudely, they're just "over-excited." It never fails to amaze me how willing humans are to excuse and rationalize rude dogs' behavior instead of teaching them good manners. Part of developing appropriate social behavior is learning that, no matter how excited you may be, there are other folks in the world and certain basic rules of politeness still apply.

During an off-lead play session at our camp, two adolescent dogs began to roughhouse at top speed, resulting in one of them crashing hard into an older dog who'd been minding his own business. With a loud roar, he chased the offender for a few steps to make his point. "Watch where the heck you're going!"

A few minutes later, with the game still going strong, we watched as that same youngster found himself headed once again on a collision course with the older dog. It seemed another crash and altercation were inevitable. To the surprise of many who were watching, the youngster used all of his skills to avoid the crash, neatly swerving past the older dog who made no comment. The puppy had learned that no matter how excited he might be by the game, he still had an obligation to be polite.

We would look with raised eyebrow at a mother who allowed a child to simply carom around a room, bouncing off people, and did nothing to calm the child, who told those her child had shoved and pushed that "he's just over-excited." Just as parents bear some responsibility for their children's actions, dog owners have a responsibility to help their dogs act in an appropriate way—not to excuse rudeness.

Sometimes, this requires that we not allow a young dog (or a dog of any age) to escalate to such a high level of excitement and arousal. As a rule of thumb, the more excited and emotional a dog becomes, the less capable he is of thinking clearly and acting appropriately. (This is also true of all other animals, including people.) Wise handlers know that when emotions are running high, a cool down period is a good choice to avoid problems. Sometimes, helping a young dog learn what is appropriate requires the assistance of a normal, well-socialized dog who can make his point without leaving anything but a clear message imprinted upon the puppy.

Normal dogs, like normal people, are often incredibly tolerant of the antics of youngsters. Tolerance level is highly individual and dependent upon a dog's experience with other dogs. Those without much experience may not be nearly as tolerant as dogs who have seen a lot of dogs come and go.

Tolerance levels are also highly dependent upon the youngster's age; there are different expectations for what constitutes appropriate behavior at any given age. What we might find acceptable behavior in a three-year old child would be frowned upon in an eight-year old. Dogs also have a timetable in their heads. Dogs under 16-weeks of age can usually take appalling liberties with an adult dog. As Dunbar notes, there appears to be a "puppy license" of sorts, possession of which entitles you to be an utter pest without much repercussion. Past the age of four months, the "puppy license" expires as hormone levels shift and psychological changes occur. At this point, adult dogs begin to gradually insist on more controlled, respectful interactions from youngsters.

"I've got the dog trainers of the class stumped, as they don't really know what to do. Cream's normally such a sweet dog, good with commands, great with people. Cream's also wonderful with children, and has an endless supply of patience with kids—they can pull on her ears, hug her tightly, pull on her tail—and Cream loves it. Cream's fine with dogs who are calm, even friendly towards them, with her tail wagging, and she might even try to get them to play."

Let's change this a little to read:

"Margaret is fine with people who are calm and well-behaved, and interacts with them appropriately. She's also endlessly patient with and kind to children, even bratty ones. But, when loud, obnoxious teenagers begin shoving her around, she's really weird—she starts telling them to leave her alone. What can we do with Margaret? Her behavior has us stumped."

Make any sense? Of course not. One of the most incredible aspects of the Cream consultation was the complete focus on Cream as the problem. Not once had the owner or instructors looked past Cream herself to find the source of her problem, although they had at least recognized "hyper, young dogs" as the trigger. While they were perfectly willing to excuse the inappropriate behavior of the rude dogs, they were also willing to classify appropriate behavior as a problem.

I found it very depressing that Lee Anne, in posting a request for help on a Golden Retriever email list, got this response consistently from the many "experts" online. "This is not normal Golden behavior. This is a serious problem."

As if being a Golden, or any other breed, somehow removes portions of the normal canine behavioral repertoire! No matter what the breed, no matter how much genetic manipulation may have muted or inhibited certain behaviors, a dog is a dog is a dog. And the basics of dog-to-dog communications remain the same: a growl means back off in any breed's language, a tail held high and stiffly is a warning, rolling over on your back is an apology, etc.

Cream was not acting aggressively; she was displaying normal canine behavior in response to considerable rudeness. She had never so much as uttered a sound toward rude dogs until they invaded her space and made contact with her. And even the most angelic of Goldens is quite capable of growls, snarls, snaps, bites, and other communications in the face of such rudeness.

My Dog is Rude?

My experience has been that owners of breeds considered non-aggressive cause the most problems in dog-to-dog interactions simply by being unaware that their dog is rude. To the owners of non-aggressive breeds, there doesn't appear to be any thought that rudeness can take many forms. Anyone can recognize that a dog lunging and snarling is being rude. Far too few folks recognize that simply getting into another dog's space—however sweetly and quietly—is just as rude in the world of dogs. Owners of rude dogs do not perceive their dogs' actions as rude; they see only "friendliness," as if the behavior for greeting people is the same as greeting another dog. It's not! Thus, the classic line, "He's only trying to say *hi!*"

A good friend of mine was a case in point. Her Sheltie was a quiet, retiring little fellow who had never displayed any aggressive behavior toward another living being. Yet repeatedly, this dog triggered impressive displays from other dogs, usually those of the

German persuasion, when he wandered into their space. Inevitably, my friend would be horrified by "those aggressive dogs" and retreat with her Sheltie, never suspecting that she and her dog were the problem.

Though charming and sweet, her Sheltie was extremely rude and invasive; the responses he got from other dogs were largely quite well-deserved, though inevitably, the Germans were blamed. In each and every class this woman attended with her Sheltie, owners of dogs who did not tolerate such rudeness had to watch her dog constantly. And in each and every class, she was completely unaware how many potential problems had been averted by alert handlers who simply moved their dogs out of her dog's rudeness zone.

There were three basic factors at work: the Sheltie's lack of dog-to-dog socialization, which resulted in his being completely ignorant about what constituted polite behavior toward other dogs; my friend's misconception that her "friendly, non-aggressive" dog could never precipitate a problem; and the freedom she gave her dog to invade the space of other dogs without any thought or understanding of how that might be perceived by dogs who were minding their own business.

She became a much sadder and wiser handler the day she unthinkingly walked her Sheltie into my pack of German Shepherds who were playing happily in their own yard. She made a few seriously bad assumptions.

First, she assumed that because they were my dogs, these six German Shepherds were somehow exempt from the nasty realities of pack behavior. No matter how well-trained or socialized an individual dog may be, when that individual becomes a member of a pack (and six is decidedly a pack), the rules change considerably. Pack behavior is a complex, often unpleasant, but very real part of dog behavior.

Her second assumption was that because each of my dogs had met her dog in the house on an individual basis, they would be fine with him as a group out in the yard. In the house under my supervision is a very different scenario than playing in the yard without my supervision.

Her third assumption was that somehow her dog would be able to cope with a group situation when he'd consistently had problems dealing with my Shepherds one-on-one.

My dogs, revved up from being in the house for hours and now playing hard, were surprised to see then come up from the direction of the barn when they'd last been seen in the house. They charged at her. Instead of lying down and crying "uncle," which was the correct response, the Sheltie tried to run, found himself at the end of the lead, and accidentally pulled up into a very upright position (read "challenging posture" in dog language).

I can only guess, but knowing my dogs, I believe that his lack of normal behavior coupled with his previous displays of rudeness made this unintentional challenge the last straw. Fortunately for all involved, my dogs had no intention of hurting him, just teaching him some basic manners. He walked away from it all with only one small wound (made much worse later when he ripped his stitches out!). His owner made her final bad decision of that day and instinctively reached into the swirling pack to rescue her dog; she was bitten on the hand.

My friend learned a lot about dog behavior that day. Although I'd have preferred some other way to educate her about what constitutes rude behavior, she was finally open to hearing how rude she had allowed her dog to be. It was a complete shock to her. She viewed her dog as a completely non-aggressive animal. Every time she had heard me speak about dog-to-dog rudeness, she had assumed that only aggressive, boisterous, loud dogs were rude. She became a much more aware and careful handler only after my pack drilled home the lesson.

A Higher Standard or Unrealistic?

Just as my friend unrealistically expected my dogs to be exempt from the ugly realities of pack behavior, Cream's owner and her instructors were unrealistically holding Cream to a higher standard of tolerance than they would expect from themselves. After all, she is a Golden. Does that mean she, or any other typically low-aggression breed, should tolerate rude dogs making physical contact?

Like people, dogs have varying thresholds for what I call the "fool factor." Consider yourself in this situation. You are walking down the street, and a group of loud, noisy teenagers—busy at the center of their own world—bumps into you and knocks you down. Do you smile at them? Do you mutter, "Watch where you're going," as you brush yourself off? Do you get quite vocal in expressing your displeasure?

All depends on your tolerance threshold. It also depends on your mood, your health, the various stresses at work in your life, etc. Imagine that you had just won the lottery moments before they bumped into you. Chances are pretty good you'd be far more tolerant than if you'd just come from a meeting with the IRS. What if you'd been mugged a year earlier by a similar group of young hooligans? Chances are good that you might view this group as potentially dangerous, again altering your possible response to their rudeness.

Our dogs are no different. Each dog—no matter what the breed—has his own tolerance threshold, and that threshold is variable as a result of many factors, including basic breed charac-teristics. Some breeds have been selectively bred to have a very high tolerance threshold because they are asked to work in large groups. Foxhounds come to mind as a breed specifically selected for tolerance of other dogs. Generally speaking, the guardian breeds, by their very nature and job descriptions, are not meant to work in groups and have a stronger sense of personal space. Thus, they are usually much less tolerant of rudeness.

Bad experiences, such as Cream had on several occasions when she was attacked by other dogs, can make a dog quite sensitive to rude behavior by other dogs. From the dog's point of view, there is the very real possibility that such rudeness could become an actual attack—it has in the past. Health problems can also affect a dog's tolerance level. A dog who is in pain (whether just muscle soreness from hard work or play, or a disease, such as hip dysplasia or the creeping onset of arthritis) will have far less tolerance than he might when he's feeling fine.

We cannot expect our dogs to be saints—at least not until we can rise to that level of tolerance ourselves. And that's unlikely to happen any time soon. We can expect our dogs to be tolerant to the degree that we educate them, socialize them, and protect them—with respect to their individual needs and boundaries.

In my opinion, Cream has actually tried hard to achieve sainthood. As Lee Anne notes, if put in a setting with dogs, Cream's response is to turn her back to them. I don't know how much more you can ask for from a dog, especially one who's been punished for saying what needs to be said to rude youngsters.

If Cream were a dog with a very short fuse and a very low "fool factor" threshold, I'd feel obligated to help her find coping skills to lengthen that fuse—if only to lower the stress in her life. Fuse lengthening is especially important if you are going to ask the dog to cope with situations that typically arise in class and dog event settings. But, where I find "short fuses," I usually find other contributing factors. So, I'd take a very hard look at the relationship between dog and handler (particularly in the areas of leadership and boundaries), and the dog's degree of self-control and socialization with other dogs.

Protecting Your Dog

Talking over Cream's story with fellow trainers I respect, one question kept popping up. "Why were these dogs allowed to jump all over Cream in the first place?"

It is an important question. To my way of thinking, a critical part of the relationships I have with my animals is this promise: "I will protect you." And to the best of my abilities, I do not violate this promise in any way.

A few years ago, I was invited to be part of a fund-raising dog walk. One of my duties was to lead the entire group on the first lap of the walk. I had chosen my oldest bitch, Vali, to accompany me. As we waited, hundreds of dogs and handlers assembled in the park. Many of the dogs were quite excited. Some dogs were only under borderline control. Vali lay quietly at my side, watching it all with great tolerance.

One particular dog caught my eye—a huge yellow Labrador who was dragging a small child behind him as he plowed through the crowd. I watched as this dog marked not only every tree or bush he passed, but also several pants legs of unsuspecting people. More aware handlers quietly gathered up their dogs and moved out of Mr. Rude's path, thus avoiding potential altercations.

As he moved closer to us, I saw Vali's head turn toward him and become quite still. Her eyes began to harden as she assessed— quite accurately—just how rude a dog this was. I could see her contemplating possible responses should the Lab be so rude as to invade her space (which in such public settings is perhaps 2–3 feet from her body). The only intervention necessary was to gently touch her on the head and say, "Yes. I see him. And you're right. He is rude. I'll handle it."

Then, I stepped slightly in front of her so that if he approached, he would have to first come through me. Immediately, Vali relaxed and went back to watching the crowd in general, though she did keep an eye on Mr. Rude. Fortunately for us, Mr. Rude veered off to hassle another dog, and the moment passed.

There were other ways I could have responded. I could have seen Vali's very appropriate response as potential aggression, and tell her harshly, "Leave it!" To my way of thinking, that does not acknowledge or respect her feelings; it merely demonstrates my own fears about losing control of my dog's behavior.

I could have ignored the subtle signs that she had some concerns about Mr. Rude and wait until he invaded her space, then punish her for defending herself against rudeness. To my way of thinking, that would violate my promise to protect those I love and then add insult to injury by punishing her for protecting herself. Keeping that promise to my dogs means that I am obligated to watch for any sign that they are beginning to feel concerned about a situation and act quickly to eliminate or minimize their concerns.

Unfortunately for many dogs labeled "dog aggressive," a weird loop begins to form between dog and handler in the struggle to deal with this behavior. Understandably shocked when their dog exhibits any kind of aggressive behavior, the handler begins to scan the world at large for anything that might trigger that behavior again. They become hyper-alert to any potential situation and, upon sighting a potential problem, grab the lead with a death grip in order to control their "aggressive dog."

Their own concern coupled with the death grip escalates the dog's anxiety and aggression, usually resulting in precisely the behavior they sought to avoid in the first place. Far more insidious, however, is the message sent to the dog whose handler pays intense attention to the world at large but none to the dog himself!

A woman presented to me her terrier Brisky with the complaint that he was "dog aggressive." Brisky had very little off-lead socialization, was quite fearful of other dogs, and all his "aggression" was nothing more than defensive offense. If given a choice, Brisky would have happily left the room and driven himself home.

The woman looked like a Secret Service agent on presidential detail; she never stopped scanning the room for potential problems. Who was going to get up and walk their dog past Brisky? Was that dog going to turn around and lie down facing Brisky? She saw potential disaster in every slight adjustment or movement of another dog. What she never looked at was Brisky himself. Consequently, his "sudden" explosions always came as a shock to her.

I felt very sorry for Brisky. He sent many signals to his owner that he was worried and afraid. But all his communications were ignored until he felt so pressured he had to protect himself in the only way he knew how. It is very hard to feel safe and protected if the person you are with pays no attention to you.

Consider this scenario. A mother and her daughter are walking in a crowded mall. The mother is hyper-alert to the crowd and vigilantly checks for potential dangers to her child. The child sees a woman who looks just like the bad witch in a favorite book. Fearful, the child reaches for her mother's hand, but the mother is so busy scanning the crowd that she ignores the child. As the "bad witch woman" gets closer, the child grabs her mother urgently. But her mother doesn't respond. The flow of the crowd forces the "bad witch woman" to pass next to the child who, now terrified, screams loudly. The mother, shocked by her child's seemingly inexplicable behavior, asks angrily, "What is the matter with you?"

What if, when the child anxiously reached for the mother's hand, she had received a reassuring squeeze and a smile as her mother looked down to check on her? What if the mother had seen the signs of concern on her daughter's face and stopped to ask, "What's wrong?" and then, seeing the problem, moved so that she was between the "bad witch woman" and the child as they passed.

In which child do you think the anxiety level will be higher: the child whose mother ignores her until she screams in terror or the child whose mother pays attention? Trust within a relationship is built on the belief that our behavior will be noticed and responded to, if not necessarily always full understood. In my experience, dogs whose owners recognize, acknowledge, and act on early signs of discomfort have deep trust in their owners' ability to protect them in almost any situation.

When working with people like Brisky's owner, my goal is to get them to watch the dog, not the world at large. If their attention is outward, instead of on the dog, they will miss the early signs that their dog is feeling uncomfortable and needs some help. The earlier the dog receives acknowledgment for what he's feeling, is helped to cope with a situation, and given evidence that you understand his concern and will deal with it on his behalf, the less likely his behavior is to escalate into dramatic displays. This is true whether it's a dog like Vali, who believes that a rude dog should be taken down a peg, or a dog like Brisky, who is afraid.

I encourage handlers to be quite active in protecting their dogs, whether that means quietly walking away to a safer area or, when that's not possible, literally stepping in physically to present the first line of defense..

Brisky visibly relaxed when his owner began watching him, not the world. By the end of the day, he was far more tolerant of situations that had previously triggered his explosions. No doubt he felt safer—someone was finally listening to what he had to say and offering him help (such as changing his body posture and, thus, his emotional state) when he needed it.

The owner reported that she felt calmer knowing that Brisky would let her know how he was feeling and that she could help him before he felt the need to protect himself. Instead of having to scan the world at large constantly, she could relax and focus only on what Brisky was telling her about the world as he saw it.

Cream's owner would not have let a rude child bang Cream on the head or hit her with a stick; she would not have allowed cruel strangers to walk up and kick Cream. No caring owner would ever let another human being do anything to their dog that would create a need for that dog to protect himself.

Yet, just like many otherwise loving dog owners, Lee Anne had done nothing to protect her dog from other rude dogs. A hefty portion of responsibility for failing to protect Cream needs to fall on the instructors.

Lee Anne, quite reasonably, looked to the instructors for guidance. If they did not intervene when a dog acted rudely toward Cream, how would Lee Anne know that she should? If they defined Cream's behavior as a problem, then Lee Anne—although upset and unable to make sense of such a diagnosis—would also begin to see a problem.

Fortunately for Cream, Lee Anne kept widening her search as she sought help and advice for her dog. Not all owners work so hard to find an answer when their heart says, "Something is not right here."

An instructor's responsibility is to educate dogs and owners and to protect each dog from the others in the class. This requires an understanding of canine behavior, and an ongoing attendance to subtleties of behavior that foretell problems brewing.

Dealing With the Rude and the Fools

During our consultation, Lee Anne asked the question that inevitably arises, "But how do I stop dogs from being rude?"

There is no easy answer to that question. Certainly, no matter how aware or dedicated a handler is, it is not possible to stop other dogs from being rude—or, more to the point, it is not possible to educate all other handlers so that they won't allow their dogs to be rude. I believe fools and rudeness are widespread, and, to the best of my knowledge, there's no concerted government program to eradicate either rudeness or foolishness.

Here's my advice for dealing with the "fool factor."

Socialize your dog thoroughly with other dogs. For dogs, choose playmates of a similar age and adults who have been well-socialized themselves. This means off-lead socialization, not sniffing noses at the end of the lead. The more experience a dog has with other dogs, the more refined his judgment will become about what constitutes rude or foolish behavior and how best to deal with it. He'll also learn how to be a polite dog himself.

If a dog has not or cannot be well-socialized, be realistic about what you can expect from him in his dealings with other dogs. This may mean altering your training or competition goals to be fair to a dog unable to cope with the stresses of these situations.

When socializing your dog under someone else's instruction or guidance, be careful. Some instructors and trainers are appalling ignorant about basic behavior and unable to set up a positive socialization situation. If you feel uncomfortable with a situation, remove your dog. It only takes a few seconds for a bad experience to leave a lasting impression, particularly on a young dog.

Just turning dogs loose together to play is not socialization. There has to be supervision and intervention when the potential for a problem appears. The instructor must pay attention to each individual dog as well as the pairings or subsets within the whole play group. If one dog is getting overly excited, it's time to gently capture him, take him out of the play group, and calm him down before letting him play again. If a fearful dog has reached his limit, it's time to remove him from the group and give him time to relax and build his courage before putting him back in. If a particular dog or dogs begins to gang up on another dog, it's time to break up the brat pack.

Instructors need to carefully assess groups and not pair dogs inappropriately. For example, a rambunctious Labrador puppy should not be paired with a timid Sheltie dog. Since Lab dogs often resemble a cannonball crossed with a Sumo wrestler on drugs and consequently like heavy-duty physical contact (preferably in mid-air, at great speed), the more sensitive Sheltie may be quickly overwhelmed and quite possibly hurt by the Lab dog. Not only might this leave a very bad impression on the Sheltie, but it can also teach the Lab puppy that rudeness is acceptable.

Watch your dog. Your dog will tell you all you need to know about his perception of the world. When you're with him, really be with him. Pay attention to his behavior.

Position yourself and/or your dog so that he is always in your peripheral vision. Practice checking on your dog often. If he appears to be concerned, find out why. Help him. Protect him.

Teach yourself to recognize the small, subtle signs that he's shifted out of a perfectly relaxed state of mind. These may be as simple as the tilt of an ear, a raised eyebrow, slight holding of the breath or tensing of the muscles. Each dog is different—learn to read your own dog.

If you can't watch your dog in a situation where there are potential problems, put him somewhere safe. I've seen far too many incidents occur unnecessarily because handlers were engrossed in a conversation or fascinated by what was happening in the ring and ignoring the dogs at their side.

When a handler's attention is elsewhere and not monitoring the dog visually, I call this handling by Braille—knowing nothing more than that there is still pressure on the lead and thus the dog is still present. Unbeknownst to you, the dog could be acting rudely himself or trying to avoid a rude dog. Handle your dog with awareness, not by the length of your lead.

Be proactive in protecting your dog. If you see a fool and his rude dog headed your way, do your best to protect your dog. If possible, walk away, lightly and quietly asking your dog to come with you. Be sure you are breathing and relaxed. Don't let your apprehension about a possible altercation impact negatively on your dog.

If you can't walk away, try to get the fool to stop. Position yourself between the fool and your dog. If necessary, loudly and firmly tell the approaching person that your dog is not good with other dogs.

In close quarters, where there really aren't any options for moving away, shield your dog with your own body. (Remember, stepping between dogs is an act of protective leadership.)

If you need to, sharply tell the fool to "please control your rude dog." You'll probably get a dirty look (fools rarely believe they or their dogs are rude and are shocked when spoken to sharply) but chances are good they'll at least make a show at controlling their dog or move huffily away from you.

DOs & DON'Ts

DON'T bring an intolerant or undersocialized dog to a puppy kindergarten or other concentrations of rudeness and stupidity when you know he can't handle puppies, stupidity, or rudeness!

DON'T put your dog in situations you and he are unprepared for.

DON'T turn a rude puppy or dog loose with an intolerant adult.

DON'T expect your dog to like every dog he meets (at least until you like every person you meet).

DON'T allow your dog to become overexcited or rude.

DON'T allow others to allow their dogs to be rude to your dog.

DON'T ignore your dog or what he tells you about his feelings.

DON'T punish a dog for telling another dog to get out of his face.

DON'T punish an adult for reminding a pup to mind his manners.

DON'T let your training or competition goals overwhelm your good sense—always be fair to your dog.

DO respect your dog's need for and right to his personal space.

DO socialize your dog so that he's wise in the ways of other dogs.

DO accept that your dog may inexplicably dislike another dog.

DO build your dog's tolerance with repeated, positive experiences.

DO educate yourself regarding normal, appropriate dog behavior.

DO plan how you will handle difficult situations, people, or dogs.

DO earn your dog's trust by keeping your promise to protect him.

DO pay attention to your dog when you are with him.

DO insist that your dog behaves politely.

DO respect that your dog's individual needs may or may not be in line with your training or competition goals.

DO put your dog first; hopes, dreams, titles & goals all mean nothing if you ignore the needs, fears & realities of who your dog is.

DO honor & respect your dog's concerns, whether or not you share them. (Remember how your mom left the light in the hall on at night when you were a kid? It probably wasn't because she was afraid of the dark.)

CHAPTER SEVENTEEN

If Only That Hadn't Happened, This Dog Would Be Fine

Understanding, explanation and rationalizations

Why are some dogs shy? fearful? nervous? aggressive? irritable? unfriendly? difficult to train? clingy? unable to be left alone?

People have many explanations for why dogs act as they do. Sometimes the dog's history becomes baggage that the human carts along for the dog's entire life. Recently, I asked someone about her dog's pulling on leash, and she began her answer with, "He was found near a dumpster when he was six weeks old." The dog was three-years old now. How does being found near a dumpster have much to do with pulling, which is an interaction between a dog and handler?

Sometimes, the human guesses at what happened. "A man with a hat must have abused her because she hates men with hats." Maybe she just finds hats scary. Or maybe she's unsure about men in general, and the hat just adds to the scariness. If a 10-foot tall three-headed slime goblin suddenly appeared on your street, your reaction wouldn't be due to having been abused by three-headed slime goblins but rather due to the strangeness, the novelty, the unfamiliarity of the thing. What is attributed to abuse in the dog's past can often be more accurately laid at the feet of being poorly socialized and, thus, having a very small list of known and familiar, but a huge list of what is strange, novel, unfamiliar and frightening. By contrast, a well-socialized animal has a huge list of familiar and known items, people, and experiences.

However, when we explain behavior, what is frequently heard is this:

"If only *that* hadn't happened, this dog would be fine." *If only that hadn't happened, this dog would be fine* is at best a faulty premise. At worst, it is a rejection of the reality that individuals vary considerably in their ability to handle whatever life dishes up.

"Would have been fine" or "was fine before X"—based on what criteria? After what kind of assessment? Breeders, trainers, rescue/shelter staff, and dog lovers alike often have no meaningful, detailed way of assessing behavior. They are not lying when they pronounce the dog as "perfectly fine," but they are reporting on an opinion based on a less than thorough assessment. Without a Geiger counter, the woods and fields around the nuclear disaster site at Chernobyl look quite lovely. Sometimes, what passes as an assessment of a dog is a lot like evaluating Chernobyl without checking for radioactivity.

Ironically, there is frequently some tacit acknowledgment that all is not truly fine. Instructions provided regarding the animal reveal a lot. This can be heard in, "Oh, just don't reach for him [or try to touch or look at him], and he'll be fine." None of these warnings indicate an animal who is *fine*, who can remain functional and appropriate and keep his teeth to himself (or stay in the same room) *even if* humans look or touch or act humanoid. Warnings exist where there is a potential for problems. Ever seen a sign that says, "Caution! Dry floor with good traction!"? No one warns,

"Careful—he will stay relaxed and happy if you look at him, hug him, or touch him."

"If only *that* hadn't happened..." often points to specific experiences that people believe are to blame for any number of behaviors and responses that are less than desirable, whether that's being anxious or fearful or shy or aggressive or intolerant or reactive.

"It's because he was flown on a plane."

"It's because he's in a shelter."

"It's because the woman reached over his head."

"It's because the man was wearing sunglasses."

"It's because he had five different people transporting him."

And so on. In the end, what is believed, is that the experience alone—whatever it was—ruined the dog.

This bears some detailed examination if we are interested in doing right by the dogs entrusted to us.

Experience can, will, *does* affect an animal. No question. But to pose experience as the thing that can destroy a stable resilient individual is not quite accurate. What one animal finds so traumatic might be simply confusing and annoying for another animal. An unexpected hug from an overly exuberant child can result in one dog just waiting patiently for it to end, while another dog in that same setting might feel trapped and frantically bite the child's face. Being hugged is not the problem. ***It is how the dog experiences the hug***. And that's the key here. Who is the individual, and to what extent does any given experience affect him?

Each individual dog is the product of genetics and developmental stimulation (also referred to as Nature) and the cumulative effect of his experiences (sometimes referred to as nurture). Which is more influential? Genes are not the sole determinant of behavior; behavior is not solely the product of experience. Though the "if only that hadn't happened..." folks like to think otherwise, there is no point in deciding *between* Nature and nurture.

In her book, *The Mirage of Space Between Nature and Nurture*, Evelyn Fox Keller points out that both are inexplicably intertwined. Each influences the other. As Keller notes, there is no understanding of a wall as purely bricks or purely mortar, just as no drumbeat exists without a drum and a drummer. There is a great illustration in her book that shows one child holding a hose aimed at bucket, and another child at the other end of the hose ready to turn the faucet on. She asks, if X number of gallons fill the bucket, which child contributed more to that? The answer, of course, is that both children and both actions (turning on the faucet, holding the hose) are necessary to fill the bucket. This, in an elegant nutshell, is the Nature/nurture argument.

Animals vary widely in their adaptability, their coping skills, their resilience, their ability to remain functional in any given situation, under any given stress. There is a huge range between the end points on the functional/dysfunctional spectrum. It is helpful to consider it as a continuum with many layers. On each layer, an animal could be closer to one end of the spectrum than he might be on another layer. For example, if one of the layers is auditory sensitivity, then a deaf dog is on the dysfunctional end of scale, though he may be perfectly functional on all other layers.

On one end of the behavior spectrum are animals with limited ability to handle stress. Their behavior can be rigid, maladaptive, inflexible, or even downright fragile. These dogs can experience poor quality of life at times due to specific stressors or stimuli (for example, thunderstorms). Or the dog may have a generalized inability to adapt that affects the dog throughout his life in many or even all situations. For such dogs, care must be taken to provide the best possible environment and lifestyle to avoid creating distress for them. It may take very little for them to find a situation upsetting or distressing. The goal for their caretakers is to support their needs so that they can function to the greatest possible degree. Sadly, for some of these dogs, they may have severely limited adaptability.

On the other end of the behavior spectrum are the animals who can adjust, continue to function, have coping skills. These animals are "take them anywhere, do anything with them!" hardy souls remaining highly functional under even extreme situations. They are able to recover quickly even from distressing experiences. Their behavior is robust, flexible, adaptive, and resilient. Typically, these animals can move easily between varying environments and a wide range of demands without any significant changes in their behavior. Since they can adapt to their environment, the environment does not need to be adapted for them.

What we need to focus on is this: the adaptable, resilient animals will have very different experiences than fragile, less adaptable animals even in the same situation. Consider a visit to the zoo's reptile house. If you're a snake lover, the reptile house is a wonderful experience full of interesting animals, and you enjoy every minute of your visit. If you're afraid of snakes, the reptile house is a frightening place that you do not enjoy and leave as quickly as you can. Same situation, two very different experiences.

When we understand that any given event *may or may not* affect the animal **depending on who that animal is**, we can stop blaming an event and begin to understand the individual animal. Then the important questions become:

How do you assess the dog's ability to adapt, function, cope?

How do you know how fragile or robust an animal is?

Assessing Functionality

One important clue to adaptability and coping skills is the ability to remain **functional.** The degree to which basic functions are disrupted tells us how much any given stress or situation is affecting the animal.

The basic functions to be considered are:

• **Eating** Functional animals eat when hungry. Variations on the spectrum range from limiting intake, needing particularly tempting or "special" foods, having to be coaxed, being hand-fed, being force-fed, vomiting, to total refusal or complete disinterest in eating.

• **Drinking** Functional animals drink when thirsty, and in appropriate amounts. Variations on the spectrum can range from excessive drinking (psychogenic or "stress" drinking, which may have to do with gastric distress) to refusing to drink at all.

• **Sleeping** Functional dogs sleep approximately 12–14 hours per day. Variations on the spectrum when stressed/distressed include hypervigilance that precludes sleep, constantly interrupted sleep, insufficient sleep, and excessive sleep.

• **Elimination** Functional animals urinate and defecate on a regular basis, with properly concentrated urine, properly digested food, and a compact stool.

Variations on the spectrum when stressed or distressed range from refusal to urinate or defecate in new (or "unsafe") conditions or only under very specific conditions (no humans nearby, no noises, no other animals, etc.), increased urination and defecation, to outright diarrhea and urinary incontinence.

• **Social Interactions** Functional animals are able to maintain their social skills under a broad range of conditions. Please note: I said *maintain,* not *develop.* An animal who is lacking social skills with either humans, other dogs, or any other species cannot be said to be dysfunctional due to circumstance; the skill did not exist prior to the circumstance.

Variations on the spectrum when stressed/distressed include avoidance of interactions, irritability with interactions (even with familiar people or other dogs/animals), clinginess, unwillingness to be left alone (when normally willing to be), to outright aggression. Each of these can be as true with familiar people and animals as it might be with unfamiliar people and animals.

• **Learning and Thinking** Functional animals can employ their knowledge and skills under a broad range of conditions. Functional people may be able to drive, perform their jobs, and cook dinner when upset. More fragile people may need to have someone drive them, call in sick, and order take out (assuming they eat!).

As the animals' stress/distress *increases*, their ability to learn and think clearly *decreases*, one notable effect of arousal.

Variations on the spectrum when stressed/distressed include slow or inaccurate responses, mild to significant inability to correctly process signals, and outright inability to learn or perform.

• **Play** Play is a high level function based on physical and emotional well-being, and, in particular, a feeling of safety in an environment and with playmate(s).

Example #1: Dog is adopted from one home to another, but, within two weeks, is brought to a boarding kennel where he spends 10 days. From there, he is adopted to yet another home. The dog has continued to eat well, drink normally, urinate/defecate with some mild diarrhea on a few occasions, interacted appropriately with all staff who handled or walked him, played when given the opportunity, and was appropriate with other dogs and cats at the facility.

Not surprisingly, this dog handled very well the journey to his new home, a nearly nine-hour trip with multiple stops and a change of vehicle and crate. Upon meeting his new people, he greeted them with a wagging tail and a pleasant attitude, and cheerfully hopped into their car for the trip home. Within a day, this dog had begun to bond with his new owners and continued to adapt without any significant changes in his functioning.

Example #2: Dog is picked up from a situation where he has lived all his life since birth. When approached by the rescuer, the dog becomes immobilized with fear. He is unresponsive to food, touch, verbal signals, and tugs on leash or collar. He must be carried and forcibly placed into crate for transport. Upon arrival at his destination, the dog remains immobile in the crate, unwilling to come out even when the door is left open. Left alone in the safe room with food and water, and observed from outside the room, it is more than three hours before he moves towards the food and water placed just inches from him. Not surprisingly, it is a long road to being fairly functional in the world for this dog and a matter of years of consistent effort and environment. He can still be pushed into dysfunction by disruptions in his schedule or unfamiliar people.

Example #3: Dog competes several weekends each month in a dog sport. The handler is careful to pack her white noise machine for the hotel room or the dog can't sleep and will pace most of the night. She also packs special foods because the dog often refuses to eat while traveling but can be tempted with exceptional foods. Her medicine kit includes plenty of anti-diarrheal medication, because diarrhea is common with this dog while traveling (though he has normal stools at home). Finally, she includes supplements meant for stress relief, because the dog often appears stressed during trial weekends. When asked about her dog, this handler reports that her dog "loves this sport and the showing adventures" they share. Not surprisingly, she also reports some performance and training difficulties with this dog. She is offended by the notion that her dog's behavior demonstrates a high degree of stress, dismissing it with, "Oh, all the dogs I know are the same way. He's fine!"

Any of these dogs could be assessed according to their ability to be functional at any or all of the points along the way—at the point of initial contact, during transport, and at the final destination. At each assessment, we need to know:

- How functional is this animal?
- Where is function impaired and to what degree?
- Is function in any area impaired sufficiently to warrant medical intervention?
- What negatively affects the animal's ability to function?
- What positively affects the animal's ability to function?

A behaviorally robust animal can adapt to a great deal before a situation becomes distressful for him. A behaviorally fragile animal cannot handle much without becoming dysfunctional. The same experience can have vastly different effects on individuals. Knowing how to assess an animal in terms of basic functions helps us be truly more humane and aids us in making the best decisions for him as a unique individual.

This functional assessment gives us a way to know where the animal stands in that moment and helps us continue to assess progress or deterioration on a fine level, as often as necessary. Functionality reflects the animal's current state. Not what he might be or what he was in the past, but how he is **Now**. The dog lives in Now. Assess him in Now, support him in Now, train him in Now.

Of Hostages & Relationships

Do you need to isolate a dog or limit playtime with other dogs or people?

He said that he loved her. He said that his relationship with her mattered almost more than anything else in his life. He said that he enjoyed working with her and sharing new ideas. To be sure, she never took her eyes off his face, paying no heed to the audience who waited breathlessly to hear his secrets for such adoration, such undivided attention.

"First," he said, "I never let her talk to anyone but me. When I leave for work, I lock her in a room, which is pretty boring for her, but when I get home—oh, is she ever glad to see me! If she wants to do anything, except go to the bathroom, she has to do it with me. I control her food, her exercise, and all her activities. Wherever we go, I insist that she always look at me, so I know for sure she's paying absolute attention. I don't let her have any friends, because they might distract her or use up the energy she needs for working. Being the only social contact she has, I am very important to her. Naturally, she'd rather be with me than anyone else."

The audience didn't gasp. They didn't protest in any way. They didn't stand up and tell him that was archaic, outrageous treatment. They did not shout out that this was not, could not be, the secret of a healthy, happy relationship. Instead, they nodded, and took notes. They thought this made perfect sense.

Was this some sensationalistic talk show featuring, "Taking a Hostage—Key to a Happy Relationship?" Unfortunately, it was not a reality TV show. This was a dog training seminar, and *he* was talking about *her*—his dog. (And, while I say "he," this attitude is certainly not limited to male trainers and applies equally to female trainers.) If this had been a man talking about his wife, or a mother discussing how she raised her kids, the audience would have been rightfully appalled. But it was, after all, only a dog, and these were techniques helpful to top competitive performance.

If we examine the theories behind the methodology, we come up with some pretty scary notions. While long appalled by the notion of needing to isolate a dog to improve his willingness to work with you, I began to wonder why this concept was not only "successful" (if, in defining success, you are willing to discard a healthy, normal relationship and focus only on competitive performance) but sounded vaguely familiar.

The answer? "The Stockholm Syndrome," a psychological phenomenon named after the people in a Stockholm bank who were held hostage. In this syndrome, those forcibly taken hostage, surprisingly, develop positive feelings for their captors.

To understand the Stockholm Syndrome, you must understand the effects of sensory deprivation. Imagine, if you can, being forcibly removed from your daily life (with all its familiar environments, routines, and social interactions) and put in a strange place from which you cannot escape. Your only interactions are with your captors, whose behavior can be capricious—that is, beyond your ability to understand why or when they may choose to do something for you, with you, or to you. They may withhold food and/or water in order to raise its value to you in order to receive your compliance with their demands. You may be left in complete silence or darkness with nothing to do, nowhere to go. You may not be allowed to talk or interact with other prisoners.

It would appear that a reasonable (human) response to this would be anger. To be sure, this is often the initial response of any hostage. Yet, as the hostages in the Stockholm bank demonstrated, the desire for survival quickly supersedes hostility. Your entire world now revolves around your captor(s), and, within the sensory vacuum in which you now exist, their moods and actions become all consuming. Anticipating their desires, appeasing them—these are the possible keys to survival. Further, deprived of normal social interaction, you begin to see your captors more sympathetically. In the original Swedish case, investigators were astonished to hear the freed hostages asking for leniency for their captors.

For any social creature (man, whales, gorillas, wolves, horses, dogs, chimpanzees, dolphins), the quickest way to create neurosis and abnormal behaviors is social isolation and a sterile sensory environment. Within the zoological community, the greatest success rates in terms of animal mortality, health, and normal breeding and rearing of offspring occurs with animals who are allowed normal social groups and interactions, and whose environments are as varied and rich as a zoo can manage to provide.

In the horse breeding community, stallions are often isolated from contact with other horses, and are notoriously neurotic, displaying self-mutilating behaviors and high levels of aggression. I have worked with stallions who were allowed to interact normally with other horses, turned out in green pastures to play, and given demanding work schedules at high levels of training. These horses were intelligent, sane, and an absolute pleasure to work with. I have also been in a barn where every one of the horses (none of them stallions) demonstrated neurotic behavior. These poor animals were so carefully protected in the name of performance in the show ring that their lives consisted of little more than being held hostage in a beautifully maintained cell.

A review of child development books and theories reveals that an important key to well adjusted, productive, and healthy children is wide-ranging exposure to a variety of people and relationships, environments, activities, and ideas. It is hard to imagine any rational person advocating that children be isolated and sensory deprived so that they could achieve better grades or respond more perfectly to their parent's desires. And it takes very little imagination to grasp what the effects of such isolation might be on the child.

Consider the concept that dogs should have limited, if any, play or social interactions with other dogs. The rationale here is that a dog dealing with another dog must either be dominant or submissive. In having to learn the rules of normal dog behavior, these trainers believe that the dogs will have their fragile egos irreparably damaged by having to submit to other dogs, or become unduly dominant, thus rendering them incapable of successful competitive work. Does this really make sense? What happened to stable dogs who can actually deal with life?

I read one article where the author carefully explained how each new group of dogs required a sorting of social hierarchy, and that if the group changed at all, the dogs would need to sort it out all over again. What a surprise! Every time you (also a social animal subject to power structures and dominance hierarchies) enter a room of other people, the same process repeats itself. It is through such repeated interactions and sorting that you come to some sense of who you are no matter what group you are in. The most confident dogs I know are dogs who are extremely well-socialized and able to handle themselves in almost any setting.

There is a grain of truth here—a very small grain at best. There is no question that an inappropriate playmate can scare the pants off a dog (especially a puppy), sometimes leaving a serious and lasting impression. There is no question that a dog who is an absolute bully with other dogs may make a lousy competitive dog—lacking respect or sense or both, no doubt he could be found wanting when it comes to respecting and cooperating with a human. But the larger truth here is that a normal dog who is properly and thoroughly socialized, allowed to develop appropriate manners, who knows when to politely bow deep and when to hold his head high, is a dog not easily shaken by odd encounters.

What these trainers fear most of all is that their dog will come to prefer dogs as playmates rather than the handler. They will even tell you this in no uncertain language. My question is, if the dog would rather play with another dog than work with you, doesn't that tell you something? If your spouse preferred to spend his/her weekends with another man/woman, wouldn't that be a clue?

Let's pretend that you adore checkers and attend every checkers tournament that comes to town. One day, you decide that your child/spouse/friend (choose one) should also enjoy checkers as you do. As you sit enraptured by the fine points of multiple jumps, your guest sees a squirrel in the tree outside the window. "Gosh," they say as they leap from their seat, "I didn't realize there were squirrels around here!" And off they go to stare up a tree, finding this much more fun than watching checkers with you. Big hint there, eh?

It is possible to have a relationship based on mutual respect, free from anything that remotely resembles sensory deprivation, and still have a dog who will work his heart out for you, and, even

more importantly, with you. Since I do not choose to compete in the obedience ring, there are some readers who, mistakenly equating titles achieved with knowledge earned, will question my basis for this statement.

In my many years of involvement with dogs, it is the two plus years of working with my dog as a Search & Rescue team that taught me the most about what is possible between a dog and a human in a working relationship. On our first official search, what few joys the obedience ring held for me evaporated in a moonlit cornfield as I watched my dog work and work and work, with me, off lead under challenging circumstances, right until the sun came up and the search was called to a halt.

I have watched my search partner, a young German Shepherd named Chilkat, play sticks and "keep away" with other dogs in the search unit as we prepare for a practice search. A quiet whistle or call brings him to me, instantly ready for work, which means a scent discrimination exercise that could last up to two hours in pouring rain, freezing cold, or blistering heat. Walking through a park with seven off lead dogs, I have sent a friend to hide and, without having to dispose of the other dogs, put Chilkat on a formal search command. He is at work in a flash, ignoring even the puppy's attempts to restart their game of a moment ago. In both cases, when his job is done, Chilkat happily returns to playing with the other dogs, groveling appropriately to his elders or giving a pesky puppy notice that her manners are somewhat lacking.

The notion of having to artificially ensure that my dogs find me incredibly interesting disturbs me. If I ever found myself in any relationship with healthy beings (human, canine, equine, or any other species) where I had to cajole, bribe, pay, or take hostage my intended pal in order to assure their interest in me, I'd have to take a very long hard look in the mirror.

In the case of unhealthy or unbalanced beings, such as very sick or emotionally disturbed animals or people, I have indeed made unusual foods, exciting games, and/or extra attention my opening bids in the friendship game. And I did so with full recognition that as they were at that moment, a normal relationship was not possible, and that I chose to interact with them in an unbalanced way. But, I did not withhold normal food, access to independent play or playmates, or my attention. That is not a relationship, or a friendship. It may be an appropriate interaction between organism and source of stimuli, but I need more from and give more to dogs than simple, conditioned responses. I have dogs first and foremost as my friends, and I do my damnedest to treat them as such. I often fail to be as generous and unflagging a friend to my dogs as they are to me. But I'm learning.

The dog is commonly referred to as "man's best friend." I wish that dogs could talk, if only to gain their perspective on what that really means for them. Perhaps, like the hostages in Stockholm, some of our dogs would find themselves pleading for leniency for their captors.

CHAPTER NINETEEN

I Had To

When explanations are justifications, who is fooled?

There are a few phrases in the animal training world that really push my buttons. When talking to trainers, the one that will always get a reaction from me is this explanation for why the trainer used a specific technique or piece of equipment that coerces, punishes, or causes discomfort or pain: "I had to."

When pushed to explain further why they "had to," it very often turns out there were other options available, but the choice was made to use that technique or equipment for reasons such as "Well, the class was nearly over" or "the client was frustrated" or "I had tried everything else" (really?), and so much more that has nothing to do with a careful analysis of the dog, the behavior, the situation, or training methodology. Worse still, the trainer often attempts to rationalize it as if the *animal* left the *trainer* no other options.

This has always bugged me, and it reminded me of something else that I couldn't quite put my finger on till I was reading a novel recently. The abusive husband justified his behavior by telling his wife that she had actually caused him to beat her because she hadn't been [fill in the blank—*attentive enough? quick enough? pretty enough? etc.*].

There are situations in which the use of force to defend yourself or another being is justifiable. Our criminal law allows for this and yet also places a burden on us to utilize any other option available to us before we use force. It would be good for dog trainers to be held accountable for their use of aversives and force in this way. I wonder what would change if trainers had to build a case for their actions, including specifics of what other options had been considered, employed and discontinued, or discarded before even trying them.

The most common example is the handler who shows up with a prong collar on an excitable dog. Watching the dog tow the handler into the seminar, I can see that the handler is a contributor to the process. After all, it takes two to tango, and it definitely takes two to pull. Dogs *never ever* pull off leash. But, as the handler stands with taut leash that is the only real connection to the dog, I consistently hear, "Well, I don't really like to use this collar, but he's so excitable, I just had to use it."

What's left on the table as other solutions to the pulling dog doesn't get mentioned—positive reinforcement, consistency in expectation for on-leash behavior, actual training for on-leash manners, appropriate handling of the lead to eliminate the handler's pulling, teaching self control, etc.

Being Accountable

Whenever I use any force, I do three things:

First, I strive to be as aware as I can be that I have used force in whatever form. My inner dialogue involves actually articulating to myself, "I am using force." No rationalization or excuses, just that statement and a mental note to review this situation and the use of force in depth.

Next, as soon as it is appropriate to do so, I then ask myself why this use of force was "necessary." Sometimes, the use of force was purely defensive, the only solution I had in that specific moment where I was taken off guard or the animal did something completely unexpected and potentially very dangerous to himself, to me or to others nearby.

But, sometimes, I'm just a jerk with low levels of patience, and I've lost my sense of fairness. Either way, I have to hold myself accountable. I hold this proverb close to my heart: *"Where knowledge ends, violence begins."*

Then, I ask myself how I got into this situation. Did I push the animal too far? Did I ignore warning signs, violate the animal's need for safety, or over-ride a threshold? Did I put the animal in a situation where his understanding and/or skills were insufficient for him to handle the situation? Had I ignored prior behavior that clearly indicated this situation was likely to happen? Am I just re-peating a past pattern for me or the animal, or both?

Whatever the answer, the solution is to recognize where **I** went wrong. *Not the animal.* Animals who feel safe, who are under their thresholds, who are not sending warning signals, who know how to be cooperative, and whose skills and knowledge allow them to cope with the situation—well, strangely enough, these animals just don't seem to force anyone to use force. Odd...

In a strange but useful way, I am the prosecutor, the defense attorney, the judge, and the jury all in one, in my role as a trainer, and I am also the defendant on trial for my decisions. Kind of a *Paw & Order* thing, because sometimes there are also detectives involved who round up all kinds of evidence that will be brought to bear.

If I've ignored past behavior which would have predicted the animal's response, then the prosecuting attorney asks quite firmly, "Why did you choose to disregard your own prior knowledge?" My defense attorney doesn't have much to say.

If I've ignored warning signals, sometimes my defense attorney can make a good case for simple incompetence: that I just was not sufficiently familiar with this particular animal to correctly read his signals. Having learned my lesson and apologized profusely, I am released (on probation!) as all involved are sure that I won't make that mistake again.

Mistakes made from judgment calls gone awry are usually forgivable offenses, provided I'm not brought up again on the same error. All past offenses may be brought to bear; no protection from having a sealed record, no prayer of having the record expunged.

I think it's a good thing for a trainer to remain accountable for mistakes past and present. Keeps me honest.

A Choice

Replacing the phrase "I had to. . ." with "I chose to. . ." puts the responsibility where it belongs—on the trainer who made the choice to use techniques or equipment. It helps us all remember that, in making that choice, by definition, we excluded other possibilities. When using force, we need to be very clear that, in discarding other options, other possible solutions, we may also be choosing to limit what is possible when we push ourselves.

Many years ago, while attempting to demonstrate some no-pulling techniques in a seminar, I was utterly exasperated by a young Labrador. Clancy had leaped up and head punched me very hard not once but twice, making me see stars and really hurting my nose.

Clancy was not malicious or intending harm, he was just an exuberant adolescent who had been taught that leaping around was acceptable. Not being physically sensitive, it was doubtful it dawned on the dog that a head butt was very painful to a human. I had been patient, kind, vaguely successful, but, by the second slam to my face, my patience began to shred. I began to think, "One good correction might get through this dog's thick skull." I surprised myself by thinking that, but then I further shocked myself (and some of the audience) when I explicitly asked the handler for permission to use a physical correction on her dog. She agreed, trusting me as a trainer to do right by her dog.

In that moment when she trustingly agreed to let me use force on her dog, a very heavy burden was laid on my heart. Not only did she trust me with her beloved canine pal, but the head butting dog also trusted me. So I found a little voice that challenged me to push myself further, to help this dog *without* force. It was like having a gauntlet thrown down at my feet. *Do it without force, without ego, without justifying force.*

With that internal challenge simmering in my mind, I decided to see how far I could go before I chose to use force. I was very clear in my mind that using force was a choice I would make, not something I was forced to do. I persevered, patiently applying the techniques I've used with countless dogs, a positive approach that does not involve pain or aversion and seeks to engage the dog's mind, not control his body. In the end, I never did use force on Clancy, and I was successful in helping him find a new way of walking on leash. His response and head butts were nothing more than a lack of knowledge and skills. How on earth could I justify using force on a dog whose only crime was not knowing how to be right?

Very few in that audience would have blamed me if I had chosen to use force. They had all witnessed how hard I'd been hit in the face by the dog's head despite careful, positive handling. They had all seen how much time I'd already devoted to trying to do things positively.

Many would have given up long before I did, as if there is a certain amount of time to be spent trying and then all hope is lost and it's okay to use force. This, in particular, makes me very sad because I work hard to help trainers learn what real patience looks like. I nearly sent the wrong message by almost going down the "I had to. . ." road.

In fact, for Clancy, my typically recommended applications of more time, more patience, and thin slices did the trick, as they almost always do. I am grateful to my inner voice that held me accountable and helped me find more patience and fresh eyes for what this dog needed.

I think about that dog, Clancy, a great deal. I have carried him for years in my heart and will continue to do so. I will keep seeing his owner's trust in my judgment as a trainer, will keep seeing Clancy's bright, trusting eyes. That inner voice that holds me accountable is also the one that challenges me to find new ways always to keep the light in those eyes, in all the eyes that turn towards me. It is my job not to betray the trust. I hold myself accountable for what I *choose to do*, and that is never explained away by the phrase, "I had to. . ."

CHAPTER TWENTY

The Habit of Excellence

"Excellence, then, is not an act, but a habit." (Aristotle)

I admire excellence in any field, whether the excellence is shown in amazing cakes or hand-painted silk jackets, in being able to fix almost anything mechanical (thank you, dear husband, for possessing that particular excellence!), in creating music that sings in my heart long after the final notes have faded from my ears. I have been privileged to watch many trainers who can create an agreement between themselves and a dog or horse that is rich with nuance and harmony.

Whatever the particular field or pursuit, what sets these people apart from others who would also bake a cake or play music or train a dog or repair the broken is this: their passion for excellence, for doing their best, always. It is the belief that excellence can always be improved upon. Those in pursuit of excellence know that learning never stops, and that ever deeper understanding is available even to an "expert" if curiosity and self-analysis are an ongoing part of the process.

There are times when our best of the *moment* is not the best that may be *possible*. Everyone I know who has achieved a high level of excellence has come to grips with this and learned how to accept it, and yet not allow that concept to limit them. A fine line lies between being unrealistically critical of our own efforts and recognizing when we have done our authentic best in that moment, even if it is not exactly what we intended. Our intentions can drive excellence if we are willing to practice in the many ways that allow our skills to match our intentions.

Dog training is a lot like life. There is no easy recipe, no formula that, if we just apply it correctly, will assure us good results. Chemistry, math, physics, mechanics—all offer satisfying ways to get it right over and over if we are careful and thorough (and if we truly understand the many variables at work). But, like art and medicine, dog training is an inexact science, no matter how diligently we try to apply the formulas of operant conditioning and learning theory. Live animals in dynamic bodies and minds make dog training an art that science can *assist*, but all the science in the world cannot create that ineffable connection we seek with our animals.

As people trying to understand and live with and train dogs and other animals, we remain practitioners, always practicing, always in pursuit of excellence. Excellence is achievable in any given moment, but it is not a destination. It is a journey of a lifetime, where each step offers us the chance to practice the excellence of that place and time.

When I found this quote from Aristotle, I thought it would be an ideal poster for any training school (or any home, kitchen, office, barn, bowling alley, cupcake bakery, etc.!):

> *"We are what we repeatedly do. Excellence, then, is not an act, but a habit."*

Practice the habit of excellence. Among the many gifts dogs bring to our lives, one of the greatest is the opportunity to continually be our best selves.

Acknowledgements

Although it is never evident to the reader, books take a lot of time to create. My books come into being because of the many talented and kind people who gave their time, skills, and help. Writers write alone, but within a safety net of love and support.

My world is held in place by my husband, John Rice, who puts up with my crazy ideas and shares me with a lot of animals and people.

For her close, considerate and lightning speed copy-editing, I'm grateful to Gisele Plourde. Many thanks to the other sharp eyed readers – Cindy, Kathryn, Suzanne, Glenn – who helped fine tune the book with their thoughtful suggestions.

Glenn Massie gets a special thanks for being the final straw, which turns out to be a good thing for a change.

Suzanne Webb's keen eye for design aligned beautifully with the photo Cindy Knowlton shot for the cover. Thank you both for bringing beauty to this book through your photos. I love knowing Swift, our cover model, added his canine creativity by striking that pose on his own.

My love and thanks to Darcy Britt, Ted Bromley, Deb Gillis, Jo Hamilton, Kathryn Horn, Gijsbert Janssens, Cindy Knowlton, Heather Leonard, Kathy Marr, Nancy Reyes, Catherine Thomas, Suzanne Webb, and Kirby Wycoff.

My greatest thanks to all who have trusted me with their best friends – their dogs – an honor that I never take lightly.

Photography credits

ABOUT THE AUTHOR

Suzanne Clothier has worked professionally with animals since 1977. She is well respected for her Relationship Centered Approach to training, as well as her many innovative contributions to the dog training world.

She travels extensively in the US and internationally teaching workshops on a wide range of topics including her innovative RCT techniques, her behavior assessment tools CARAT and RAT, and the Enriched Puppy program.

A consultant to several service dog organizations, she has also taught for groups as varied as Wolf Park, Alaskan Dog Mushers, and Association of Pet Dog Trainers, the University of Minnesota's Nature Based Therapeutics *"Speak!"* conferece, and as keynote speaker for many national breed club conferences.

Collaborating with Dr. Kirby Wycoff, Suzanne is the co-creator of **The Reflected Relationship**, a new model for animal assisted therapies and interventions placing goodness of fit and respect for the animals as central to any humane, ethical engagement of animals to benefit humans.

Her book, **Bones Would Rain from the Sky: Deepening Our Relationships With Dogs** has received wide spread praise from every corner of the dog world, including twice being included in the Wall Street Journal's list of Top 5 Dog Books. An award winning author of videos, books, booklets and numerous articles, Suzanne has written articles for the AKC Gazette, Dog Fancy, Dogs In Canada, Off Lead, Clean Run, Wolf Clan and breed magazines and newsletters around the world.

Since 1994, her website has offered a wealth of information through her free articles, and now her YouTube channel offers free videos as well.

She served as a committee member for the AKC's Agility Advisory Board, and as a committee member of the American Humane Association's Task Force for the Development of Humane Standards in Dog Training.

Suzanne lives on a working farm in upstate New York with husband John Rice, and their considerable animal family of dogs, cats, parrots, tortoises, horses, donkeys, Scottish Highland cattle, pigs, chickens and turkeys.

A long time breeder of German Shepherds, dogs from her Hawks Hunt line have been successful in many fields – agility, obedience, tracking, herding, Rally, Search & Rescue, therapy work, guide work, nose work and of course, as beloved family companions.

Also by Suzanne Clothier

BONES WOULD RAIN FROM THE SKY:
Deepening Our Relationships with Dogs

*"Clearly, this is a book written by someone who truly understands
and loves dogs. All dog lovers will want to read it."*
Jane Goodall, author of *Reason for Hope*

BONES is a book like no other, taking the reader on an exploration
of our relationships with dogs that moves far past the recipes of how-to
books or mere technicalities, and into the very soul of relationship.

Whatever your involvement with animals, **BONES** will change forever how you view the profound, intimate relationships that are possible
when we truly open ourselves to another.

DVDs

AROUSAL, ANXIETY AND FEAR: Empathy, Understanding
& Options for Anxious or Fearful Dogs

Is your dog just a bit shy? Stressed? Afraid? Wish you knew how to
help? This two hour presentation by Suzanne Clothier provides detailed
information to help viewers develop empathy, understanding and humane options for working with stressed or anxious dogs.

Whether you're wondering about counter-conditioning vs. flooding,
if your dog might need medication, or if training would help, Suzanne
provides a thoughtful framework for finding the best solution for each
individual dog.

www.suzanneclothier.com

INTRO TO RELATIONSHIP CENTERED TRAINING
Understanding your relationship with your dog is fundamental to effective & humane training. This video is for anyone seeking new perspectives on life shared with dogs, anyone who wants deeper understanding. RCT puts the relationship at the center of all you do with your dog. And that can change everything.

YOUR ATHLETIC DOG: A Functional Approach
Originally released in 1995, this groundbreaking video was ahead of its time, going beyond the traditional structural approach to look at functional movement. **YOUR ATHLETIC DOG** remains accurate, timely and helpful to any serious handler, offering a systematic approach to gait analysis, and massage, stretching & vet approved exercises. Includes a 100 page workbook.

More

RCT TRAINING GAMES (with Heather Leonard)
Features 24 delightful games, perfect for developing real life training skills in group classes. Each game can be played at five different levels, from beginner to advanced. Suitable for mixed age and mixed skill groups, **RCT TRAINING GAMES** are perfect for creating games classes.

BOOKLETS
* **Understanding & Teaching Self Control** The need for impulse control is a foundation in all training
* **Finding A Balance: Issues of Power in the Dog/Human Relationship** Finding a respectful balance that meets dog & human needs
* **Shifting Shapes, Shifting Minds: Body Posture & Emotions** Examines the relationship between a dog's emotional state and his body posture
* **The 7 Cs** A little gem that looks at seven simple concepts
* **Following Ghosts with John Rice** A practical guide to the tracking relationship

Find us on Facebook
www.suzanneclothier.com
FREE articles, blog & monthly newsletter